the stay-at-home
MARTYR

Also by Joanne Kimes

Pregnancy Sucks
Pregnancy Sucks for Men
Dating Sucks
Dieting Sucks
Grammar Sucks
Potty Training Sucks
Bedtime Sucks
Breastfeeding Sucks
Christmas Sucks
Menopause Sucks

THE STAY-AT-HOME MARTYR

A Survival Guide for Having a Life Outside Your Kids

JOANNE KIMES
and JENNIFER WORLEY

gpp
life

Guilford, Connecticut
An imprint of The Globe Pequot Press

GPP Life gives women answers they can trust . . . expert, reassuring advice on relationships, health, parenting, and passions.

GPP Life is an imprint of The Globe Pequot Press.

Photo on p. iii © Jupiter Images

Spot art courtesy ClipArt.com

Text Design by Libby Kingsbury

Library of Congress Cataloging-in-Publication Data

Kimes, Joanne.
 The stay-at-home martyr : a survival guide for having a life outside your kids / Joanne Kimes and Jennifer Worley.
     p. cm.
  ISBN 978-0-7627-4942-3
  1. Mothers–United States. 2. Housewives–United States.
3. Motherhood–United States. I. Worley, Jennifer. II. Title.
  HQ759.46.K56 2009
  646.70088′640973–dc22

                                            2008024636

Printed in the United States of America
10 9 8 7 6 5 4 3 2 1

To Emily, my first, last, and most delicious pancake. I love you.
J.K.

For Ella, Iris, Leo, & Charlotte, the four people who have inspired me to great acts of Martyrdom, given me the joy of knowing life's deepest love, and offered me a glimpse into the minds of the criminally insane.
And to winemakers everywhere.
J.W.

Acknowledgments

To Holly Rubino, who inspired the idea.
And to Joanne's husband, Jeff, her biggest fan. And Jennifer's
husband, Dave, the one she knows would come and bail her out if she
ever finally lost it.

Contents

Prologue

Attention, mommies! We wrote this book in hopes that it would inspire you to care about yourself again. To love and appreciate yourself without feeling guilty or being shot down by the ruthless uber-mommy brigade. We know that somewhere under that old T-shirt, sweatpants, ponytail, and mismatched undergarments lives a sexy, interesting woman who's begging for a night out. We know you're tired. We know you can barely remember life before babies. We also know that somehow in the process of becoming a mother, you lost yourself. Every day, hour, and minute have been reduced to a single purpose: your darling children. What's wrong with that? A lot. And we'll attempt to explain why in the pages to come.

We have taken the liberty of naming this affliction, because without a diagnosis, there can be no remedy. Like any other addiction, Stay-at-Home Martyrdom can never truly be "cured." And recovery isn't instantaneous. Reclaiming ourselves as adults with valid needs is a lengthy process, filled with relapse, denial, and "start-overs." But we can't give up. We must support each other in our quest. For this reason, we have formed M.A.M.A.R.Y.—Mommies Against Martyrdom and Raising Youths-who-can't-cope! We're here to stop the spread of Martyrdom. To combat complacency. To relocate kids back to the bottom of the family food chain (where they actually feel more secure and cared for). And while we're at it, to free the world from the dreaded skinny jean and other cruel, unflattering fashion trends.

Who are we to lead this march? We are loving, overworked mothers ourselves, and we know just how deep mother/child attachment runs. We also now realize how dangerous too much love without limits can be. Between us we have a master's degree in child development, a teaching credential, five children spanning in age from one to eleven, two neglected husbands, one overweight dog, three deceased goldfish (let's take a moment and bow our heads for Gold, Gold, and Gold), and an entire Home Depot Garden Center's worth of near-dead houseplants. (See "Other Living Creatures" in Chapter Seven.) We have spent countless hours trudging through the monotonous world of the stay-at-home mother. We have observed, we have read, and we have talked serious smack with hundreds of other Martyr-mommies in peril.

Knowing how little energy and time you have (or think you have), we have tried to make this process as simple and straightforward as possible. All you have to do is read.

You may be wondering, "If I manage to get a minute to myself (which I won't because my children need constant, age-appropriate stimulation and unfaltering supervision), why on Earth should I spend it reading this book?" Here's why. Your children treat you like a doormat. And even worse, you treat yourself like a doormat. It's time for your "start-over." So put down your homemade baby food grinder and fifty-pound designer diaper bag, and let's go to it.

Chapter One

The Stay-at-Home Martyr

If you ever looked through the want ads hoping to find a fulfilling job, never in your wildest dreams would you consider applying for one that reads like this:

Wanted: *Stay-at-Home Martyr*

"Hard-working person needed to toss dreams, aspirations, and sense of self out the window in order to provide constant care for needy children. Duties include wiping up repugnant bodily emissions, fostering self-esteem in others, constant cleaning that will be immediately undone, and problem solving that could include but is not limited to infantile bargaining, blackmail, public tantrums, and high-decibel wailing. Applicant must own large, unsexy vehicle with too many cup holders and ample trunk space. Must be willing to cut close ties with friends and family and suffer severe marital discord. This position offers no pay, yet candidate is expected to fork over money for countless overpriced, unnecessary child-related consumer goods. Experience not necessary, but ability to convey resentment and selflessness simultaneously is a must."

Before having a child, you'd never willingly apply for such an outlandish job, but now that you're a mother obsessed with "proper" parenting, you're smack-dab in the middle of your own mommy cubicle, surrounded by millions of other Stay-at-Home Martyrs performing the same menial tasks for their young demanding bosses. Day after day, you deny your own needs, and those of your family and friends, to give to your children, thinking that doing so is in their best interests. You'll perform this job seven days a week, twenty-four hours a day, for the next eighteen years (maybe even longer since their resulting warped sense of entitlement prevents them from taking an entry-level job below a CEO position with full expense account).

You ask yourself why you do it. Why you give up everything you are and everything you know to cater to your young's every desire. Why you deny yourself the simple pleasures in life, from a few hours to yourself to a delicious meal with your husband, for fear of neglecting your kids and traumatizing them for life. How did we, an educated nation, wealthy with convenience and luxury, wind up at the mercy of our offspring? How did we go from putting our own needs first to sticking them at the bottom of an endless list of tasks to do for the kids, the house, and the pets? And oh yeah, the husbands.

Admit it. Whether you like it or not, you may be a member of the newest phenomenon called Stay-at-Home Martyrs. Like other recent phenomena such as super genes and diet potato chips that cause rectal leakage, a Stay-at-Home Martyr is a product of our times. But how did she evolve and how can this epidemic be stopped? In the pages of this book, we'll attempt to answer these, plus other questions like "Where do I begin?" "How do I get over my guilt?" and "What the hell is in those chips that make my colon go so crazy?" Yes, if you can muster up the courage to put down that pop-up book and read something without pictures or chunky pages, you just might learn a thing or two about the Martyr behavior. Where do we start? The beginning of course.

Parenting through the Ages

Once upon a time parents were the boss and the kids obeyed their every command with fear and without question. Depending on the era, if children misbehaved they would be smacked and sent to their cave, pueblo, barn loft, or Upper West Side brownstone without any supper. Up until a few generations ago, the belief system was that "children should be seen and not heard" and kids were darn clear that, in the family hierarchy, they were about as significant as the gum stuck underneath their parents' shoes. Parents addressed kids with a generic "you boy" or "you girl" and thought it best not to kiss or hold their infants in excess, or not at all. Why parents didn't attach emotionally with their children is up for debate. Some think the high infant mortality rate kept parents at arm's distance. Others think it was because people generally lived in fear, regimented by religious communities, and with difficult living conditions that made things like family unity a luxury. But perhaps it was simply because parenting without disposable diapers and handheld video games was too much for any parent to bear. Whatever the reason, moms and dads were in charge and children did what they could to avoid the wrath of the adult world.

The 1950s marked a mild turning point. Parents still ruled the nest, but there was more family togetherness. Ozzie came home to an impeccably dressed Harriet and sat down to a pot roast dinner around a family table. Beaver and Wally had strict rules to follow but felt free to offer their carefully and respectfully worded opinions. "Gee whiz, Mom, do I have to give back the money I found at the baseball diamond?" Sure, Mom may have been doped up on Valium and Dad secretly wore dresses late at night, but everyone held tight to their very clear family roles. You never heard Wally dish out the now-popular, "You're ruining my life!" or sneak out in the night with Eddie Haskell to chug Robitussin and hold his breath 'til he fainted. Homes resembled idyllic Norman Rockwell scenes, families stayed together, and everyone shuddered when Mom unloaded a lethal "wait 'til your father gets home."

Things took a dramatic turn in the hippie generations of the '60s and '70s. Freedom and equality were all the rage, and children became more of an equal on the family playing field. For the first time ever, they were allowed to speak their minds and become a respected part of the family—probably due to the fact that Mom and Dad (whom they preferred to call by their first names) were too stoned to really care. Parents no longer viewed themselves as authority figures and rejected the idea that discipline and limits were good things. Besides, with both Mom and Dad in the workforce, who'd be home to enforce the rules anyway? How could little latchkey Parsley, Sage, Rosemary, and Thyme achieve their full creative and spiritual potential if they were constantly thwarted by "The Man"? Free love created freeloaders with a sense of entitlement as huge as Mama Cass's ass.

The pendulum continued in this misguided direction, and now it has become perfectly acceptable to have the children in the driver's seat while parents are locked in the trunk. Kids rule the nest, and it's the parents who do as they are told. They'll sleep in their children's rooms if requested. They will short-order cook whatever meals are desired. They'll even wipe their first grader's ass if need be, until the kid outgrows the fear of his own butt crack. Parents don't hit their children anymore or, heaven forbid, send them to their room without any supper (a properly balanced diet is crucial to good health). Parents have lost the nerve to say no, worried that their child's fragile self-esteem will forever be scarred. So, instead of equipping them with a sturdy tool belt and rugged boots that will enable them to thrive as grown-ups, parents run ahead, carpeting every precious step their children take, cushioning every fall, and bailing them out of every predicament. It's no wonder that we're stuck with a generation of kids who feel entitled, get whatever they ask for, and need parental aid for proper anal hygiene up to grade school. And we have a generation of moms who are overwhelmed, underappreciated, and suffering from a nasty case of butt-wipe carpal tunnel syndrome.

> **Parents have lost the nerve to say no, worried that their child's fragile self-esteem will forever be scarred.**

In the Beginning, There Was a Lightbulb Moment

Before you went forth and multiplied, you were hip, stylish, and positively scintillating. You wrestled with quandaries like which sunglasses framed your face better, whether you should do cardio or weights, and whether to uncork the Pinot Grigio or the Grenache. You slept well at night and showered 'til the hot water ran cold every morning. You looked toward the horizon with bright eyes, shiny hair, optimism, and a sense of adventure. Then came the decision to start a family. The possibilities excited you. You pictured yourself with a beautiful baby smiling on your hip (think Violet/Shiloh/Suri/Apple), not missing a single stride as you and your husband continued your life as it had always been—sushi dinners, weekends antiquing, and Sundays spent sipping soy macchiatos on your Restoration Hardware chaise lounge chairs. You were not going to be one of those people who changed after having kids. The baby was just going to have to man up and join the party.

You spent nine months being treated like Mother Nature herself. From outlandish cravings at 2:00 a.m. to long, indulgent foot rubs, your every wish was the world's command. In the hospital, your husband fed you ice chips like grapes, and brushed the bangs out of your eyes with pride. The doting nurses praised your stamina during delivery and squirted your overtaxed nether regions with warm, soothing water. Flowers and balloons arrived to commemorate a job well done. You were a star.

At home, friends and family were desperate to see your baby, and "ooo-ed" and "awww-ed" at its glorious beauty as if you gave birth to Michelangelo's *David*. They cooked you meals, gave you painkillers, and eased you down on your inflatable donut pillow. Weeks passed and the caravan died down. Your husband returned to work, your mother-in-law flew home, and you realized for the first time that you were alone with *a baby!*

A couple of things can happen in this critical lightbulb moment. One woman will take a look at that squirmy little creature and sprint for the workforce, clear that she is cut out for a different kind of labor. Another woman, so emotionally disarmed by the arrival of her child and the fact that she hasn't taken a dump since the one on the delivery room table, loses all sense of self, and is reduced to little more than a bottle-warming, diaper-disposing automaton.

The spotlight shifts away from her and now shines brightly on her baby, and things will never be the same. What she failed to realize when she dreamed up this romantic threesome was that she would not simply be adding a baby to her existing life, but rather the baby would be adding her to his. After a few weeks of colic, crying, and sleepless nights, the baby has taken the lead role and Mom is little more than an extra with no lines. With only her stack of baby books to educate her, she stands alone, responsible for this newest member of the human race, and is overwhelmed by what that means. She becomes paralyzed with fear, afraid of doing anything wrong that could have life-altering repercussions. So, instead of taking the lead in her child's life, she is led by him. If he cries, she has failed him and needs to right her wrong. When she can't stop his crying, she cries as well, struck by the realization of what having a baby truly means. And even though she would never admit it to even her closest friend, at times, she misses her old life so desperately, she regrets having a child at all. Her power weakens as his becomes stronger. And that's when the problems truly begin.

Birth of a Martyr

The result of this new child-centered universe is the Stay-at-Home Martyr. She's not evil in her intent. She aims to help and please and nurture and succeed. Her heart is pure, but her methods are flawed. She has mistaken indulgence for love, and given away the power she needs to be effective. She's a victim of herself, and is secretly mad at everyone else because of it. She puts her kids' needs ahead of her own, which at first glance appears divine and selfless. But what she's really done is push everyone, including herself, to the back of the food line while her kids stand at the front, stuffing themselves like Augustus Gloop.

Her husband misses his old wife. A woman who laughs, has outside interests, and talks about things other than the firmness of their child's morning bowel movement. A woman whom he could hold without fear of being covered in baby yuk. He would never admit it though. Imagine the resentment of the Martyr who has sacrificed *everything* for her family! How dare he wish for a wife not covered in regurgitated sweet potato?! Such utter selfishness, such shallowness!

Her family can't bear the thought of listening to more complaints about how she just can't do *anything* because of the kids. How can she possibly (go out to dinner, read a book, plan a party, take a vacation, get her hair done, carry on a conversation) when the kids need her so?! The extended family that lives far away is constantly reminded that traveling with children is a major inconvenience and it would be better for everyone if they came to visit. But stay in a hotel. And don't bring any of their small children who might contaminate her own.

Her heart is pure, but her methods are flawed. She has mistaken indulgence for love, and given away the power she needs to be effective.

Her old, childless friends don't speak "mommy" and are tired of the myriad excuses she's come up with to avoid all social contact (and she's written them off as self-absorbed anyway). Her new Martyr friends are equally self-sacrificing and only add fuel to the ravaging fire by never expecting anything from each other. Like a gaggle of unkempt groupies, they trail after their kids to endless events, cheering wildly for every coo, every poo in the toilet, every mediocre cartwheel and missed basketball shot. It's amazing how many run-down, overweight mothers will spend countless hours and hundreds of dollars carting their children to competitive sporting events, beauty pageants, and auditions, but will do absolutely nothing for themselves.

The Stay-at-Home Martyr pushes away everyone and everything that reminds her of her former life. She resides alone on her island, where only other Martyrs are welcome to visit, but only for a short time, of course, because there are Baby Einstein classes to attend and organic raspberries to buy. Her husband is welcome too, but only if he's willing to talk solely about proper parenting techniques and details about the latest recalled toy. Once he starts talking about the office or, God forbid, his own needs, she pushes him away. The Stay-at-Home Martyr lives a lonely existence, and this loneliness inevitably leads to a whole slew of problems.

Admitting You Have a Problem

Maybe all this talk has struck a chord in you. You see yourself reflected in every word and are comforted to finally have a name for your affliction. You've known for some time that you were getting lost in the process of raising your children, but you thought a woman's life was supposed to end when her child's life began. You realize you may need help, but there is no Betty Ford Center to treat this condition (because no true Stay-at-Home Martyr would dare leave her kids to focus only on herself).

If you don't recognize yourself, perhaps you're in desperate need of a wake-up call. Someone to grab you by your overall straps* and make you announce to the world, "My name is [insert name here], and I'm a Stay-at-Home Martyr." You scoff, quite sure that this isn't you, but either you picked up this book because it resonated with you, or someone close to you gave it to you as a "gift." Let's take

---

*Overalls went out of style close to two decades ago and show no sign of returning to the catwalk, yet you find they're now your permanent uniform, believing they conceal your pregnancy weight gain. See "Out with the Old, and In with the New You" in Chapter Two for help.

a quick glance at your hair, shall we? Is it coifed, or is it dreaded unintentionally like that of a Rasta Mahn? Let's talk undergarments: Control top panties or drives-him-out-of-control panties?

Complete the following quiz and then we'll argue about just how close you are to giving Joan of Arc a run for her money.

The Quiz

1. The last phone call I received was from:
   a) My significant other.
   b) Social Services.
   c) My child's "Junior Asian Cooking" instructor.
   d) Wouldn't I love to sit down and have a phone call. Or just sit down.

2. The average price for a pair of my child's shoes is:
   a) $10 to $20.
   b) Whatever's on clearance, no matter what size or if they're both left feet.
   c) We make our own shoes together out of sustainable bamboo pulp. I let him paint them himself, and if he doesn't want to wear them, he doesn't have to.
   d) About five times more than mommy's, if I ever buy shoes at all after spending so much on soccer cleats, toe shoes, and European Richter's for the baby.

3. My last sexual encounter was:
   a) After a glass of wine and our romantic (weekly) date night dinner.
   b) I'm doin' it right now!
   c) Because we understand the critical nature of sleep patterns in young children, my husband and I do not engage in any noise-making activities after 7:00 p.m.
   d) Exactly nine months before our little angel was born, but that's okay, it's not about me anymore.

4. The last thing I read was:
   a) *Anna Karenina* and *Pride and Prejudice* . . . I just can't put either one down!
   b) I'm readin' it right now!
   c) *Jorge Curioso* (*Curious George* in Spanish) and *Wei-Wei's Kite* (with Chinese characters). We are raising our child to be multilingual and sensitive to the global community.
   d) I haven't slept through the night in half a decade. How on earth am I supposed to focus on reading material?

5. If you open my nightstand drawer you will find:
   a) A flashlight, mini fire extinguisher, photo album, *Anna Karenina, Pride and Prejudice,* and a discreet "toy" I won at a friend's birthday party ten years ago.
   b) Is a mini-fridge a nightstand?
   c) We rearranged our bedroom furniture and set up the "Nature's Best" co-sleeper where my nightstand used to be in order to promote positive attachment.

I find not having my reading glasses, lamp, aromatherapy candles, or books nearby really help me focus on my child.

d) You'd have to ask my husband, he's the only one who sleeps in there. Our baby refuses to sleep if I'm not on the floor next to the crib. Spinal atrophy is a small price to pay for a well-rested two-year-old.

6. The last thing I said to my husband was:
   a) "I love you."
   b) "Oh shit, where's the baby?"
   c) That wheat is a likely allergenic food. He disagreed. Obviously, the baby was napping and not listening to us discuss things in such a heated manner.
   d) I'm sure he has no idea.

7. You're having a playdate and your child bites another child. How do you react?
   a) I tell my child a firm "no" and show him that his friend is crying. Then I apologize like mad and send a carefully worded note the next day.
   b) "What?! He likes to play wild hound. And he didn't break skin."
   c) I would calmly lower to eye level with my child and explain, "Honey, I see that you were really enjoying your game until William tried to play with your favorite wooden truck. You looked frustrated when he took it. Maybe we should put this truck away so that you won't have to feel that way." (Hands him a

wooden ring.) "Here's a biting ring. Next time you feel frustrated I want you to bite this."

d) It's my fault. I'm sure he's a biter because I only let him breastfeed for three years and two months.

8. My morning grooming ritual includes:

a) A hot shower, daily facial, seasonally appropriate moisturizer, a quick coat of makeup, a blow dry and style. (Unless it's Friday when I substitute loofah scrub for daily facial.)

b) If I don't have time to shower, plenty of dark eye shadow distracts from greasy hair. Who knew an empty Jacuzzi tub could be such a great playpen?!

c) A simple rinse and dress. I avoid all heavily scented cosmetics because I want my infant to be comforted by the familiarity of my natural body odor.

d) Singing the alphabet twice while brushing teeth, going potty, washing hands, and if I'm lucky I can manage a couple of braids or a cute clip. Oh wait, you mean *my* grooming ritual? A baby wipe shower and some extra-strength gum are all I have time for.

How you scored . . .

a) The Golden Parent

If you answered mostly "a," you probably lied on most questions and are in serious denial. So go back and take the damn quiz again. And this time tell the truth because no one is watching and you need to get in touch with your inner Martyr. If you answered mostly "a" and were honest, then you're a glowing example of a parent. A model for us all to emulate. Hell, you should've written this book. You're a doting wife, a concerned friend, an accomplished intellect, and have great hygiene on a regular basis. So, hooray for you! But we still think you lied.

b) Hands-off Parent

The hands-off parent needs to wake up and smell the birth control. You need to stop raising the roof and start raising your kids. The whole "if-it-don't-kill-'em" attitude may work in certain cultures where young children need machete skills to survive in the wild, but the only thing this approach gets you here is irresponsible little a-holes that end up wearing an orange jump suit and picking up trash on the side of the freeway. That said, there is something refreshing about a parent who lets her children fight their own battles. Let's just make sure they have proper problem-solving skills and not heavy artillery.

c) Helicopter Parent

If you answered mostly "c," you're what we refer to as a "helicopter" parent. You have hovered and obsessed yourself into a downward tailspin. You try so hard to stay on top of what's cutting edge in parenting that you've literally stayed on top of your poor suffocating child. Back off and try to fail more often. Instead of reaching for the latest guide to "raising uber-children," reach for a stiff appletini.

d) Stay-at-Home Martyr

If you answered mostly "d," you are (without a doubt) a Stay-at-Home Martyr. Don't bother re-counting your results or switching a couple of answers. You know it and we know it. You LOVE to blame your mood and your appearance and the general state of your less-than-thrilling life on the fact that you are a full-time mother. And while we will never argue that motherhood is a tough and mostly thankless job, you are a big fat complainer. (We didn't mean that you're physically fat, though chances are you still have a couple pairs of maternity pants in the rotation.) Now before you get angry and toss this book in the Salvation Army pick-up pile . . . read a little bit more. Please, for the sake of your husband and children and the raw potential you still have in you—read on.

Chapter Two

"Glamour Do" or "Glamour Don't You Ever Look in the Freakin' Mirror?"

Picture a world where men go weak in the knees for curvy, mushy moms with droopy breasts and ruddy complexions. Where two-in-one shampoos reign, and thin women binge on pizza to try to expand their small, firm butts. Gyms would fail and donut shops would prevail. *Cosmopolitan* would take a back rack at the newsstand to *Suburban* magazine, headlining articles like "Top Ten Robes of the Season," "Scrapbooking Your Way to the Top," and "A Skinny Girl's Guide to Packing on the Pounds." Centerfold models in hair scrunchies and sweatsuits would recline promiscuously surrounded by cheeseburgers and fries!

This would be a welcome world for our Stay-at-Home Martyr. She chronically neglects her appearance for the sake of her kids. How could she possibly leave this precious child to go off and have her roots done or go clothes shopping? And with so much laundry to do for the baby, including the hand-washable items such as the cashmere baby blankets and woolen, embroidered onesies, rarely does Mommy get to throw in a load of her discount clothes for herself. She ponders how many baby stains on her shirt she can get away with and still leave the house? Thong underwear is replaced with granny panties. Makeup is abandoned. And how can she begin to find time to work out between Ice Princess Rehearsal and Toddler Tae-Kwon-Do? After years of not sleeping, shoveling in whatever her kid left on his plate while doing eight other things, and having no time available to rally what's left of her looks, many women simply give up.

> Thong underwear is replaced with granny panties. Makeup is abandoned. And how can she begin to find time to work out between Ice Princess Rehearsal and Toddler Tae-Kwon-Do?

But it doesn't have to be that way. This chapter is filled with plenty of ideas on how a Martyr can evolve into a "hot mama." To feel pride in her appearance instead of discomfort that comes from wearing a too-tight waistband and old shoes still in her pre-pregnancy size. To get her looks and health back on track so she has the energy and confidence to be all that she can be! Sound exciting? It kinda is. So put down that forkful of mac 'n' cheese and see how you got into this mess in the first place.

From a Positive Pregnancy Test to a Negative Self-Image

There was a time when you took pride in your appearance. You may not have ever had a subscription to *French Vogue*, but you probably avoided wearing dirty undergarments and stripes mixed with floral. Perhaps you occasionally sought help in the areas of hair color, nail color, and "seasonal overgrowth." You enjoyed a new purse, had a gym membership card, and sucked in your stomach when you checked out your reflection in the windows. As annoyed as you were when construction workers howled, "Chicky, chicky, chicky!" as you passed, you secretly reveled in the power you held over men. And remember your husband? Those early days when you deliberated for hours over what to wear, and recounted verbatim your entire date for your best friend, your mom, your sister, and then your best friend again. He wanted you, and you loved it.

As we all well know, priorities change once you pass your pregnancy test. It's a gradual process of deterioration that gestates and consumes like pregnancy itself. In the first trimester you ran to A Pea in the Pod and bought expensive maternity jeans and a fitted Michael Stars tee. You were convinced that you'd barely show, like one of those supermodels who, in their ninth month, look like most women do after eating Thanksgiving dinner. You quickly ordered *Pilates for Pregnancy*, bought the big rubber exercise ball, and envisioned toning and bouncing all the way to the delivery room.

By the second trimester, you'd already gained all the weight you were supposed to gain in nine months, plus a few extra pounds for good luck. Your $200 jeans dug uncomfortably into the very center of your protruding midsection, so you threw on your biggest pair of drawstring sweatpants and pronounced them your official uniform.

Not a day went by when people didn't ask if you were carrying twins, or look at you with the same expression they did when gawking at a traffic accident.

By the third trimester you were sure you'd hit rock bottom. Your days included little more than waddling, peeing, nesting, and peeing some more. But you still felt reassured by the dream that when pregnancy passed, you'd reclaim your title as a fashionable woman (or, as they say on the street, a "milf").

The time finally came to give birth. And whether it was due to the team of strangers who witnessed you pushing out what seemed like the biggest bowel movement of your life, your general dislike for every square inch of your postpartum body, or the fact that you're so busy with the baby you don't have a moment to yourself, you just don't give a shit anymore what you look like to others. With the baby now on the outside, you have far bigger fish to fry.

There was always an excuse for putting off getting back into shape. You couldn't diet when you nursed because it made you too hungry. You couldn't find the strength to exercise when you were up all night with the baby. Weeks turned into months, months into years. And now so much time has passed, and your cupboards are so full of tasty treats you buy for your kid, that diet and exercise are ideas as far out of your radar as a "spa weekend" or "eight hours of uninterrupted sleep."

This doesn't mean there's no hope for you. If you're self-conscious enough to look in the mirror and say, "Wow, I really look like hell," then you have already cleared the first hurdle toward remedying the situation. But if you still think we couldn't possibly be referring to you, despite the fact that you haven't worn a belt since you saw the plus sign on the EPT, allow us to be a bit more specific. For those of you Stay-at-Home Martyrs whose ability to communicate has been reduced to cutesy rhyming words and infectious songs, we thought we would try to make this section easy-breezy for your poor, tired brainy-wainy to understand. So we modeled it after that addictive song you'd sing to your baby to teach him the names of his body parts (before the other kids his age learned them of course):

Head, Shoulders, Knees, and Toes

DISCLAIMER: Many of these tips to improving your situation involve leaving your child at home. We know that leaving your baby with anyone other than yourself is an extremely hard thing to do. There isn't a Supernanny out there who can make organic broccoli-tofu puree as good as yours. We wish we could wave a magic mascara wand and cure you of your questionable grooming habits, but ultimately it's better that you learn how to separate now. You'll be doing your child a favor by showing him that the world does not end when Mommy leaves the room. And you'll be doing yourself a favor by feeling like a separate adult entity, even if only for an hour. For help picking someone, see "Hiring a Sitter" in Chapter Five.

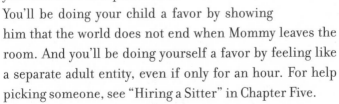

Head

(We are not referring to the thing you haven't done for your husband since you downed that bottle of champagne on your honeymoon, but rather everything that happens above the neckline and therefore the first area seen that begs for improvement.)

Skin: The skin on your face is ripe for neglect. What was once primped and pampered with three-step lotions and occasional professional facials doesn't get more than a passing glance while brushing your teeth. No true Martyr has time for such selfish acts as a slow-drying mask or a ten-minute steam treatment. In fact, the only moisture your face ever receives comes from the few errant tears of frustration you sometimes fail to suppress.

You should apply sunscreen religiously, which shouldn't be a problem since you already buy it in bulk and apply it generously to your child in case he passes by a sunny window.

Not only has lack of attention affected your skin, so has the ordeal of pregnancy, which may have left your skin blotchy with melasma. Delivery didn't help matters much. Pushing out something the size of a broiler chicken through something designed to fit an OB tampon may have left your face speckled with broken capillaries. That's why it's important to know the skinny on setting the skin straight.

I'm guessing that upon entering your neighborhood drugstore, you head straight for the sippy cup section hoping that there's been a breakthrough in spill-proof technology. It's time to expand your aisle boundaries. To hide facial imperfections, find the concealer aisle, STAT. Concealer is a great invention of our time, like salad in a bag and shelf bras. With a few dabs of this wonder product to hide imperfections, and a bit of foundation to smooth out uneven skin tone, your skin will be flawless. Also, to brighten up dull skin, scan for lotions containing the magic ingredient "retinol." No, dear Martyr, retinol is not the thing in your eye that lets you spot a miniscule hangnail on little Tommy's pinky (yet strangely doesn't allow you to notice the gunk underneath your own nails). Retinol is a brilliant concoction that literally melts away the top layer of your skin. Keep in mind that when using retinol you should apply sunscreen religiously, which shouldn't be a problem since you already buy it in bulk and apply it generously to your child in case he passes by a sunny window.

Hair: The Stay-at-Home Martyr is notorious for her poorly maintained hair. She clings to the collegiate idea that long hair makes everyone look younger. She thinks that hair color can be touched up annually, and makes the horrible mistake of wondering, "How hard can it be to trim your own hair?" Let us clarify two things. Just like the gynecologist doesn't do her own pap smear, a woman should not cut her own hair. It's much harder than it appears, and it's a slippery slope of trying to get things even, which ultimately leads to pixie bangs and a trip to the hat rack. The second thing needing clarification is that there is a glaring difference between intentionally grown-out roots and neglected roots. While grown-out roots may look good on heroin-chic models like Kate Moss, they do not look "intentional" on a woman wearing a Disneyland sweatshirt and pushing a Graco DuoGlider.

Most Stay-at-Home Martyrs we know don't blink at spending pockets full of cash on their children's haircuts (and subsequent you-did-such-a-good-job-sitting-still toys). Even their dogs rank fifty-dollar trips to the groomer (and subsequent you-were-such-a-good-boy-Fido chew toys). But does Mom take herself to the salon and buy herself a you've-been-such-a-wonderful-mother high-quality shampoo and conditioner set? Of course not. She would much 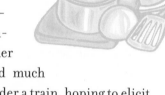 rather sigh and throw herself under a train, hoping to elicit the sympathy of anyone passing by.

And enough already of the Martyr's permanent hairstyle of a pulled-back ponytail. Even a pony gets his hair brushed and braided from time to time. Plug in that hair dryer, turn on that flattening iron, and spend at least five minutes a day focusing on your hair. What, you say? You don't have the time? Sure you do. Just spend a little less time on your daughter's morning hair routine. Clip on two or three fewer barrettes and a little less glitter gel to complement her princess outfit of the day, and you'll have plenty of time for a quick blow dry.

Shoulders

(Starting from below the neck to what's left of your abdominal region)

The first thing that comes to mind when discussing the effects of motherhood on the body is what the hell happened (and is still happening) to your breasts. It's a wild and rocky ride watching them expand, shrink, rise, fall, and then fall some more. We've heard older women joking about things such as "flat pancakes" and "ski jumps" but never quite understood the emotional journey of a woman and her boobs. It doesn't help the situation that most mommies fail to get proper support from the get-go. When buying a bra, go to an undergarment specialty store, get yourself measured, and purchase one that actually fits! The back shouldn't ride up, the shoulder straps shouldn't dig in, and it should allow your breasts to fall mid-range between your shoulders and your elbows. If it's fullness you're after, look for a padded one that can fluff up those pancakes into Belgian waffles before your very eyes. And remember, bras are like toothbrushes and need to be replaced periodically! Once they lose their give, go get some more!

The next postpartum problem is the dreaded "muffin top." For those of you who are imagining a high-fat breakfast treat that comes in flavors such as banana nut, blueberry, and apple-cinnamon, this section is for you. The "muffin top" we refer to is the flap of skin and fat that hangs over the top of your pants like the top of that baked good. It's the area referred to colloquially as the "spare tire," or "love handles." This isn't an easy beast to fight. With muscle laxity, stretched skin, a poor diet, and no time for exercise, it's an uphill battle to rid your waist of this assault. Few women are inspired enough to do the thousands of crunches required to shed it, and many

of those who actually do are still left with saggy skin, an unsightly c-section scar, or much dreaded stretch marks.

In general, the words "midriff" and "motherhood" do not mix. If you have a "muffin top" and agree that some baked goods should be kept private, use caution when reaching for the candy you hide from your kids up on the high shelf. Longer and looser shirts are your best bets. If you need to wear a more fitted top, wear it over a slimming undergarment. You'd be amazed at what these things can do. Products like Spanx and Lipo in a Box are the secret to many Hollywood starlets' hourglass figures, and are the best-kept secret next to the mysterious lover in Carly Simon's song "You're So Vain." A longtime friend of ours refuses to exist without her body slimmer undergarment. She's grown so accustomed to it that it's doubtful she even recognizes that it isn't part of her actual body. She claims that in the right lighting and from the right angle, the bodysuit looks like the creamy, flawless skin of a baby.

Layers are a brilliant and easy way to cover up stomach flaws and make you look instantly more cultured. We are referring to cultivating the *je ne sais quoi* of a sophisticated woman who turns the heads of men and women alike. Picture a woman who tosses her loose hair confidently, her imported bag thrown casually over her shoulder, her long unbuttoned wool wrap and colorful thin scarf blowing gently behind her. Now imagine the same woman, walking down the same street, only this time wearing an Old Navy v-neck tee and cargo pants. Why are we immediately drawn to one and not the other? One significant reason . . . layers.

To clarify, we are not referring to layers for warmth. Fashionable women are willing to become overheated for the sake of their outfit. Everyone knows that the practical thing to do on an eighty-five-degree day in October would be to take off the 50 percent wool pashmina. But if you've actually gotten it together enough to wear a friggin' pashmina for the day, DO NOT take it off! Instead, roll down your windows and drag your kids to Starbucks (which reminds them that they're not, in fact, the center of the universe) to cool down with a Caramel Frappuccino. Remember—make the environment adapt to you, not you to the environment!

Between Your Knees
(We use this term because we thought if we actually said "vagina," you would react violently from post-traumatic birth disorder.)

When they say pregnancy can take away your girlish figure, they were absolutely right. And you can't get more girly than your "woo-hoo," your "va-jay-jay," or whatever other pet name you like to call your crotch. If you endured a vaginal delivery, you may be worried about the aesthetics of said "battle region." After childbirth, especially if you had an episiotomy, your nether regions may look like vaginal roadkill. But time and plenty of sitz baths really do heal all. Sure, things may not line up like they did before, and it might look as if your labia suffered a mild stroke, but it's a small price to pay for having a baby. Right? Yes, right.

Also, be grateful for elasticity. True, during labor your vaginal area dilated to the circumference of a DVD, but it's since recovered. Or at least you should tell yourself it has. And if your husband is smart, he should never tell you any differently. Besides, after months (or years in some sad cases) of abstinence or ultra-careful coitus, your husband will be so thrilled to actually have sex again, he won't utter a word if things aren't as tight up there.

Although technically not your vagina, there is a part of your "down there" area that may still be suffering aftershocks from childbirth. For starters, you are way too young to be incontinent. A woman under sixty should feel free to sneeze and belly laugh after a super-size Diet Coke. Second, if you didn't follow your OB's Kegel exercise instructions during pregnancy, you definitely should now. Just raise that elevator up "1 . . . 2 . . . 3 . . . 4 . . ." and down "1 . . . 2 . . . 3 . . . 4 . . ." Repeat ten times. It's an easy thing to do while you sit in the carpool pickup line, the waiting room at the pediatrician's office, and the mom bleachers at junior basketball league. In fact, get inspired and cheerlead the other Stay-at-Home Martyrs in a "Kegel wave" across the stands.

While we're on such an intimate part of your anatomy, let's go even further and discuss the Art of Bonsai, or as it's known in the personal grooming world, "trimming the bush." We know many women prefer to "let themselves grow" and let nature take its course. And that's fine, especially if you suffered a bad episiotomy and are left with an unevenly stitched "Franken-crotch." But even if nobody ever sees you naked again, you may be a happier woman if you get in the habit of "tending the garden." Maybe it's because a woman enjoys knowing a secret. Maybe it's because it reminds you of a younger bikini-clad you, who lounged unabashedly on the beach, flirting with boys and working on your tan. Regardless of the amount of lower body traffic you support, you have a couple of options on how to tidy things up.

The first is a trip to the wax lady. After one too many razor stubble disasters and being reminded of Robin Williams' back every time you see yourself in a bikini, it's time to join the "Brazilian bikini wax club." We won't lie to you. It hurts, and it isn't fun. But it's quick and strangely invigorating. The women who perform this service couldn't care less that you're naked and lying bare ass in bad lighting. If you pick someone experienced, she'll chat casually and finish before you even know you've been flipped upside down and your legs are over your head. (This gymnastic-like event only happens with the Brazilian wax. If you prefer a more conservative and less aerobic removal, simply ask.)

If you're painfully shy and can't even begin to comprehend stripping down for a woman with a bowl of hot wax and cold hands, you can still improve things dramatically with cuticle scissors and a pair of tweezers (buy Tweezerman brand and you'll never go back). This is the one and only area where we give you permission to cut your own hair. Trim away. Get creative. We actually know a couple of women who view this chore as something of an art form. They sculpt, they prune, they shape. While this may not rank in the fine arts category with watercolor landscapes and Shakespearean theater, it is important. A little "whore-ticulture" is good for the sex drive, which in turn is good for the marriage. And a happy marriage makes a happy family.

Toes

(And by "toes," we also mean the thighs, calves, and feet. In sum, the entire lower extremity.)

When you were in the third trimester of pregnancy, you didn't give your legs a second thought. With your belly so large, you couldn't even see the damn things anyway, let alone be bothered to actually shave them. But now that your baby's been born, it's time to get those legs back in fighting shape. We know pregnancy may have done some pretty nasty things to your southern hemisphere, namely left you with more cellulite, stretch marks, and a handful of varicose and spider veins. But don't fret. There are some ways to glamour up those gams.

Although there is no cure for cellulite and stretch marks, you can make them less noticeable with a daily tanner. We're not referring to the old QT potion that turned us all a sexy shade of Oompa-Loompa orange. There has been a magnificent breakthrough in the faux tanning world, and now you can buy daily skin lotions that slowly add that much-needed hint of color. Slather it on after your (weekly) shower and watch yourself transform into someone who looks like she spends time outdoors. Not only will stretch marks seem to fade, but with darker legs, you may even look a few pounds lighter.

If your overworked veins are an issue, make an appointment with a dermatologist to see if your spider and varicose veins can be treated with lasers and injections. Usually three to four treatments, six weeks apart, should do the trick. For deeper varicose veins, the treatment is more complicated. There are several ways to get those legs back on their feet in no time, just talk to your doctor.

About your feet. We realize that for all practical purposes, your feet are functional tools to stand and walk on, and your toes serve as reliable second hands that can grab anything from dropped pacifiers to the shoulder strap of a speedy crawling baby. We're sure the last thing that keeps you up at night is whether or not your heel is cracked and calloused. It may be true that in the greater scope of life and all of its suffering, your calloused heel may be inconsequential, but your husband still recoils when it brushes against him in bed at night. Fungal infections are not sexy. Bunions don't inspire great passion. There has never been an "Ode to Toe Jam" or a ballad to "Calloused Lovers." And while you may argue that feet just don't matter, there is an undeniable attraction that comes with a smoothly shaved, tanned leg, a soft foot, and pearly polished toes.

And while we're on the subject of feet, those old-man hairs that grow out of your big toe can be dealt with in one of two ways. The quick and more painless route is to give them a once over while shaving your legs, although if you believe the old wives, they'll grow back like giant sequoias. You can also try plucking them so your toes will stay smoother longer, but we'll be honest, it can hurt more than the Brazilian wax thing.

And finally, while we're on the subject of your legs, we feel it's our duty to warn you about the greatest fashion faux pas of our time: tapered ankles. Do not, under any situation, wear tapered ankle anything. We mean it. Nothing. We would like to personally bitch-slap the person who brought

Do not, under any situation, wear tapered ankle anything. We mean it. Nothing. We would like to personally bitch-slap the person who brought back the "skinny jean."

back the "skinny jean." Sadly, most of us did not inherit said "skinny gene" and would like to respectfully request that all versions be banned for the public well-being indefinitely. No one looks good with skinny ankles supporting a wide trunk and torso. Okay, if you happen to have the build of an undernourished twelve-year-old girl, then maybe you can pull it off. But for the sake of ending an insulting fashion trend, please refrain. Conversely, we would like to thank the genius who invented the boot cut. Mr. Wide-Ankle, Ms. Flare . . . you have given us hope where there was none. You have expanded our lower legs in a way that makes us not look like upside-down triangles.

Let's Get Physical . . . Don't Panic, We Don't Mean Sex

Now that we've discussed the individual aspects from head to toe, it's time to focus on the overall package and the basic human need of daily exercise. We all know, and continually try to forget, that we require a minimum amount of exercise to prevent ourselves from becoming that half-ton guy who had to be airlifted out of his house and hauled on a flatbed to gastric bypass surgery. It's a mixed-up world where a three-month-old baby gets carted to My Gym classes weekly, but a thirty-five-year-old woman with back pain hasn't attended an exercise class since leg warmers were in style.

We admit the idea of exercising is a daunting one. Any true Stay-at-Home Martyr will protest the thought based on her belief that carrying around her first grader because he refuses to wear shoes is exercise enough, thank you. Besides, there isn't a moment free for indulgent things like working out when her day is so full tending to her family's needs (*heavy sigh*). Even if she admitted she could be more fit and did manage to find the time, working out is way too expensive. How dare she be so selfish when the Montessori school just upped their tuition rates?

But if you're a Martyr who admits she needs to get moving, here are some work-out routines that fit any budget:

> ### Price key
> *Explained in Martyr Known Stroller Priced Equivalents*
>
> $ Garage Sale Umbrella Stroller
> $$ Combi Savvy
> $$$ Peg Perego Travel System
> $$$$ Bugaboo Frog

$ Quick Fixes

· **Park at the far end of the parking lot.** We all circle the five parking spots closest to the entrance of a store a hundred times, determined to keep trying until someone leaves. Instead, park at the back where things are peaceful and there are wide-open spots to fit your extra-wide load (we're referring to your minivan, not your ass). Maintain a brisk pace while walking in and out, and carrying bags and pushing a stroller only ups the fat burn. This may seem worthless, but if you add up all the ins and outs of the day, we bet you'll get *at least* thirty minutes of cardio.

· **Always take the stairs.** It's a great way to tighten the tush, burn fat, and practice any self-defense moves you've learned over the years. It's also a great way to avoid the germs of a hacking old lady in the elevator and that awkward silence between floors that no one seems to know how to handle. If you're carting a toddler as well, all the better.

· **Use your baby for weight.** Place him on your chest when you do crunches. Hold him in front of you and lift him up and down to strengthen arms. Lord knows you spend enough on him in cloth diapers alone, so it's time for him to earn his keep!

· **Don't be a spectator.** Get up and move. When you're at ice skating lessons, throw on some rental skates and make a fool of yourself. When at soccer practice, jog around the field as many times as you can. When you're stuck in the bleachers and can't get a sweat going, at least do your Kegels.

$$ Exercise Videos/ DVDs

This is not our recommended method of getting back in shape. There are too many distractions at home, and you just can't get a good Tae-Bo side kick going when you're worried about clocking your quick toddler in the head.

But if *Buns of Steel* is the only way you're going to put down that Hostess Honey Bun, then get yourself a couple of good videos or DVDs. And if you don't have a pair of three-pound weights lying around, a pair of thirty-two-ounce formula cans will do the trick.

$$$ Join a Gym

While we're sure it'll be challenging for you to find a gym with a day-care center that's been adequately hosed down with Lysol and staffed with ER doctors, it is possible. Many gyms offer reliable child-care centers that'll give you a much needed break and an hour to reconnect with your glutes. (Reconnect with a friend, too. A workout buddy is a lovely thing and, according to research, even more effective.)

$$$$ Personal Trainer

Buy a pack of ten workouts, and the spending guilt alone will force you to get off your smushy tushy. Your husband will also be moderately angry that you spent such a bundle (this will also serve as a good motivator to get you out of the house). To deal with his passive-aggressive remarks, remind him that exercise boosts sex drives and saggy rear ends alike. And we probably wouldn't mention how strong, toned, and hands-on your new trainer Dale is.

Whatever option you choose, the important thing is to get moving. Bodies in motion stay in motion. You'll be amazed at how different you feel after just a few short weeks of improving your grooming habits, body,

and diet. Once you've raised your heart rate and shed a few pounds, it's time to address the packaging. You no longer get to plead ignorant, neglected Stay-at-Home Martyr. You are a priceless heirloom, and no halfway tasteful person would wrap a Rolex in a paper bag. It's time to take the next step and clean out your closet!

Out with the Old, and In with the New You

You spent hour upon hour readying your nursery closet for the precious arrival. Bibs were folded and neatly stacked. Pottery Barn gingham baskets filled with boiled monogrammed pacifiers, French butt balm, and vintage-appliqued burp cloths lined the shelves. Chenille blankets were fluffed and stored, and the soothing scent of Dreft detergent wafted skyward. It was as if a nation awaited the birth of a prince.

Cut to your closet. Between the pile of festering laundry tossed on the floor and the shoes that you've thrown on too many times without socks, something smells funky. And while you may argue that a shirt soiled with spit-up can be rubbed down with a baby wipe and declared clean, we say no. Bodily emissions are not acceptable fashion accessories. Even cute baby ones that remind you of little Willy's first meal of mashed peas and jarred meat. And while Monica Lewinsky may have never washed away Clinton's bodily fluid from her dress, you have our permission to wash your loved ones' out of yours.

Hygiene aside, the clothing selection available in your closet after years of blimping up and slimming down reeks of garage sale. It's embarrassing. Anyone who has had a child knows that it's difficult to lose that dang baby weight, but there's no reason that you should be wearing maternity clothes to your first parent-teacher conference. A clean closet is like a fresh, spring day. It's the mark of a woman with hope and style and an empowered attitude that cries, "I don't wear crappy clothes." As true as it is that you are what you eat, it's equally true that you are what you wear. It's time to bust out a bundle of Hefty bags and start purging.

> While you may argue that a shirt soiled with spit-up can be rubbed down with a baby wipe and declared clean, we say no. Bodily emissions are not acceptable fashion accessories.

You may feel like you don't know where to begin. You may have opened your closet door many times, stared at the mountain of maternity paneled pants, double-digit sizes, and clothes you haven't worn since you thought George Michael was straight, digested the task at hand, and quickly shut the door. This is unacceptable. We want you to call upon your inner Tasmanian Devil (or chug two Red Bulls) and go to town. Start with the obvious. Quickly toss out anything you haven't worn in the last two years. Five years for those of you who cling to every lumpy cardigan like it was handmade by your blind great-grandmother. Then, and this may be the most important

step, throw out anything that makes you feel like a big, fat, unattractive cow when you wear it.

Once you've dumped at least half of what is ailing your closet and donated it to some unfortunate country where your clothes will hopefully be shredded and made into blankets for orphans, it's time to restock. This requires careful steps. We're not encouraging a spending frenzy that will hurl you into marital counseling and simply replace your old ugly clothes with new ugly clothes. There are guidelines to follow; simple guidelines that can be adopted by even the most fashion-challenged Stay-at-Home Martyr. We are also by no means an authority when it comes to clothing, so we have gathered a few easy-to-apply slimming tips from a Hollywood wardrobe stylist and a few ridiculously fashionable people who are mostly childless or gay.

1. Buy looser clothing. It's always better to go up in size than to squeeze into a size that's too small. When buying pants, don't worry about the waist being too loose. Just be sure they fit the widest part of your body and have the waist taken in.

2. Choose clothes that elongate your look, like a jacket or long cardigan that hits just below the butt.

3. Don't chop yourself in half with color. Pair darker colored tops with darker colored bottoms.

4. Be careful of your pant length. Crop pants don't work for everyone, including shorter people whose feet barely touch the floor when seated on the toilet. Wear a shoe with a bit of a heel and pants that cover them to, again, elongate your appearance.

5. A good-fitting bra is your best friend.

6. Summer dresses and skirts that hit just above the knee can hide a multitude of sins.

Doctor You Up

When no amount of diligence will fix your physical situation, it may be time to call upon the medical community. As seen on some riveting episodes of *Dr. 90210*, many women get plastic surgery to help repair the damage done by pregnancy and childbirth. Whether it's a breast lift, implants, tummy tuck, or laser treatment, there are things that even the most steadfast exerciser can't repair. Sure, in a perfect world we would all be appreciated for our new maternal bodies and would look upon our "battle wounds" with pride instead of disgust. But the reality is, if you hate yourself enough, the risk of going under the knife starts to sound less frightening. And a little Percocet never hurt anyone (except that growing number of people addicted to pharmaceutical painkillers). As shallow as people may think you are for taking such extreme measures, it's important to remember that "if Mommy ain't happy, no one's happy."

Now that we've sufficiently poked and prodded every aspect of your appearance, don't think you can just eat a carrot, throw on a cardigan, dot on some lip gloss, and call it a day. This is only the (fruit-juice sweetened) icing on the (barnyard friends birthday) cake. Without a healthy mind-set, you'll be back to wearing your pajama pants to the grocery store faster than your eighteen-month-old can scale the side of his crib and climb into bed with you.

Chapter Three

Martyr-Dumb

Something curious happens when you have a baby that's never talked about during prenatal visits or in any of the pregnancy guides. Having children makes you stupid. Yup, stupid. It happens slowly: You forget basics, you confuse simple things, and you have difficulty forming an opinion to the point where deciding between paper and plastic becomes a mind-wrenching debate as difficult as the Israeli/Palestinian conflict. You stay at home with a drooly, cranky, needy kid who wants constant care, and you are one brain cell away from being deemed criminally insane. These days we don't always have family around to help out, and hiring a teenage babysitter who does nothing but check her e-mail, text message, and eat you out of house and home will cost you more than your husband earns. It takes a damn village to raise a kid, and all you have is yourself (and occasionally your mother-in-law, who may actually require more maintenance than your infant).

Our brains are so deprived of sleep and full of irrational worries that it's a miracle we can make it home from the market with all our groceries and our children. To make matters worse, we're constantly inundated with parenting tips and pressure to become uber-moms. And the scary thing is that all of this is okay with Ms. Martyr. She may be two IQ points shy of a loaf of rye bread, but she's willing to be a zombie as long as she can channel what's left of her brain stem into being a perfect mother. She can't just lay out a box of cereal and call it breakfast. She has to grow her own organic berries so her toddler will understand the principles of photosynthesis and buy cereal with the right balance of soy-protein and probiotic yogurt cultures. For her older children, she willingly sits and hot-glue-guns a three-dimensional model of a California mission while they argue with her about why it's okay to wear two-inch wedge heels on P.E. day. And all this before 8:00 a.m.

Too many women are on the verge of a complete mental breakdown. They have no recollection of thought before they had children, and risk forever existing in the infantile world of ABCs and addicting Barney songs. You may wonder, "If I've really become such a moron, how will I even know if I've sunk to such a level?" Here's a simple guide, a benchmark for sanity. Refer to it when you're so desperate for adult interaction that you find yourself waiting to chat with your pool guy. And he may not even speak English.

You Know You're Getting Dangerously Close to the Edge When . . .

· You snap out of a trance while driving on the freeway, realize you've passed your exit, and have no idea what you've been doing for the past fourteen minutes.

· You repeatedly lose your car keys and then finally locate them in places like the microwave, the medicine cabinet, and the foot of your baby's sleeper jammies (which would explain why she cried for two hours straight while trying to fall asleep).

- You find yourself sexually stimulated by either one or both of the Zoboomafoo brothers. You don't know which one's which and that makes it even hotter.

- You find yourself defending the mother who went crazy and drowned all her kids in the bathtub.

- You find yourself talking in third person during sex. "Ooh, Mommy likes that. Good touch. Make nicey-nice to Mama . . ."

It's not entirely your fault. You're immersed in a world that doesn't value the intellectual growth of Mommy. It's up to you to fight the decay, but first you must identify the reasons it's happening.

Kids Are Boring

There. We said it, and it feels so goooood. It's an unwritten law that mothers should never admit things like this, but doing so is very freeing. Let's all stop pretending that spending the day with our young is nothing but hours of laughter and mental stimulation. Going into the deal, we imagined our sweet little wonders would endlessly entertain us. We'd stare at them entranced, as if gazing into a roaring fire or watching a great episode of *Lost* where they finally answer some gnawing questions. But the truth is that babies are as dull as dirt. It's no wonder you're going batty. You're so dedicated to being Supermom that you force yourself to sit for hours on end and play mind-numbing games like our personal favorite, "Wa-Wa-in-the-Bowl" (put a few drops of food color in a bowl of water. Baby splashes, then spills water and cries. Clean up mess and repeat until you want to shoot yourself in the head). You're sure that if little Violet has to play alone for more than twenty seconds, she'll suffer from lack of stimulation, grow up feeling neglected, do poorly in school, and ultimately marry someone she doesn't love so that she'll never be alone, all to make up for that blip in time you left her by herself.

While we're on a roll, let's be brave and admit that some of us don't like to play. Many of you will think this is a sad and horrible thing. But truth be told, we are both the "set-stuff-up-for-my-kids" kind of mom, not the "get-down-on-the-floor-and-make-believe" kind of mom. The thought of sitting at a Little Tikes picnic table, playing restaurant, and nibbling on Lego tacos for hours makes us instantly depressed. Fairy-princess wedding party? Suicidal. Constant playing is boring for anyone old enough to have grown breast buds. But still, millions of moms get down on all fours because innately, we are givers.

Our dear Stay-at-Home Martyr is baffled. "How can I *not* play?" Her child demands that she play Monster Truck Madness with him from the moment he wakes up until his lunch and subsequent Mommy-n-Me Karate class. She simply isn't allowed to have any interest other than him. So she spends her whole day catering to his every whim and, as a result, is exhausted and (deep down inside) resentful that she has no time to herself. If your child is used to you hunkering down for the afternoon to build a two-story marble maze while he snacks on the gluten-free brownies you made, you'll have your work cut out for you. He'll need to be weaned off you like a tweaker off meth. Stand strong and be prepared for monumental outbursts and emotional "You hate me!" or "I'm so bored!" performances that would rival the dramatic roles of Meryl Streep.

There are two important things to keep in mind. One: It's okay to say no to your child. Not just *okay*, it's *imperative* that you say no. If "no" is too hard for you, try a "not a chance," "forget it," maybe a nostalgic "when pigs fly," or an all-time classic "over my dead body." Little Emma needs to know that you're the adult and she is the child. You're the Queen Bee and she is the worker. She'll feel safer knowing that you have distinct limits and are capable of enforcing them. She also won't be as devastated when she enters the adult world and finds that people deny her all the time. Bosses, boyfriends, teachers, law enforcement officials who ticket her despite her flirty tank top and batting eyelashes. It's better that she learn humility from you and not from a bitter highway patrol officer working the night shift after your darling's first annual "poor judgment" college party.

The second thing to remember is that learning to play is a vital skill. It develops imagination, inner dialogue, self-confidence, reliance, and motivation. Children who are left alone to play are interesting, imaginative, and don't whine incessantly, unable to come up with a single idea on their own. Children who know how to play will scurry past you (as you work fastidiously on your Italian mosaic

> It's okay to say no to your child. If "no" is too hard for you, try "not a chance," "forget it," maybe a nostalgic "when pigs fly," or an all-time classic "over my dead body."

table), dressed in a tablecloth cape and high heels, claiming to be the dread pirate veterinarian who saves puppies and kitties lost at sea. This is the sign of a healthy imagination. This is a child who will have good critical thinking skills and be able to get himself out of a bind by looking at a situation from all angles. He may also be a kid who embarrasses you at the bank by pretending to stun the teller with his saber because he's an ugly alien guard out to destroy planet Earth. But that's the price you pay for creativity.

This isn't to say that you should completely ignore your kids. There's value in joining their games and bonding over a fun trip to the Cabbage Patch Hair Salon. But there's also value in saying, "Go outside and find something to do before I go all 'Mommy Dearest' on your ass." (Of course, you may choose to reword this, and if your child is small enough to be picked up by a hungry coyote, you may choose to rethink the sending him outside alone thing, too.)

If you step back a little, you'll not only give them a chance to thrive but also give yourself a chance to breathe, do the laundry, pay the bills . . .

To ensure your kids will stay busy long enough for you to drink a soda and get through a pile of mail, make sure you're always equipped with a cupboard full of interesting supplies. We're not just referring to crayons and construction paper. Keep your arsenal well stocked: sticky foam shapes, glue, pom-pom balls, fabric scraps, colored foil, popsicle sticks, scarves, dramatic play sets, wooden blocks, etc. You'd be amazed at the innovative forts, houses, spaceships, and wolf dens kids can make out of a couple Ikea boxes and a few paper towel rolls. Rotate materials so they aren't staring at the same old Fisher-Price barn every day, and if you buy creative materials, they will use them over and over. You don't have to spend a lot of money on toys either. A bulk-size box of tampons is great for stacking into cabins and rivals any Lincoln Log set we've ever seen.

You may not be able to imagine a world where you're not the sole provider of your child's entertainment, but we assure you that your children are more than capable of having a good time without you. If you step back a little, you'll not only give them a chance to thrive but also give yourself a chance to breathe, do the laundry, pay the bills, and maybe even remember what it was you dreamed about before the kids arrived.

Worry Wartyrs

Since fish crawled out of the evolutionary pond, women have been caring for their children, mostly under circumstances far more grim than today. Prairie-mommies fought off wild beasts while today's mother combats lice. Now, we scrub down the grocery cart handle for fear of cold germs, when historically women feared the plague would wipe out their entire family. Why are we so exhausted by the day-to-day care of our children when we're showered with convenience and modern-day medicine? Today's threats are far less severe than those of yesteryear, but we take them just as seriously. To put things in perspective, and in hopes of calming a health-crazed Worry Wartyr, here is a list of past and present mommy concerns.

Worries of Moms Long Ago vs. Worries of Today's Mom

Then: What if I lose my child to a pack of carnivorous wolves?
Now: What if I lose my child in Wal-Mart?

Then: What if my child gets scurvy from having no produce nine months out of the year?
Now: What if my child refuses to eat flaxseed oil? Everyone knows how important a diet high in omega fatty acids is!

Then: What if my child doesn't learn to read in our one-room schoolhouse and winds up working the mines with his pa and dying at a young age?
Now: What if my child doesn't master phonics by age four and ends up in the developmental kindergarten class?

Then: What if my children don't survive the long winter?
Now: What if my child's Patagonia fleece doesn't keep him toasty enough in ski school?

Then: What if my child dies from a polio outbreak?
Now: What if my child develops an attention-deficit disorder as a result of the preservative used in vaccines?

We know that today's world seems like a scary, dangerous place to raise our children. Part of us wants to pack up our kids and hunker down in a nice Amish community far away from Internet porn, drunk drivers, and those freaky-ass Bratz dolls. But since we show no signs of loading up the horse and buggy (and we know a real Stay-at-Home Martyr could never exist without an audio-video baby monitor), it may be helpful to try to squelch the fear of catastrophe that seems to have taken over the planet. Worry about things worth worrying about. As much as you thrive in your position as master puppeteer of the family, you may need to let go a little. All this paranoia only exacerbates the demise of the contemporary female psychology. (Mommy translation: The yucky feeling in your tummy only makes you more of a silly dum-dum.)

Poo-poo Pee-pee: A Person Cannot Survive on Monosyllabic Repetition Alone

Another reason you've intellectually sunk into an abyss of stupidity is that your communication skills have been reduced to that of a cave person. Before you had kids, you were a college grad and busy executive capable of balancing budgets and creating ad campaigns. You were witty, insightful, and cared about things that happened outside the parameters of your playroom. Now, every sentence you say either rhymes or is composed of monosyllabic words (i.e., "Mama go nigh-nigh, okey-dokey?" or "You want wa-wa for drinky-winky?"). Your singsong approach to

> You're not the friggin' Queen of England. Please stick with first person and teach your child how most of the population converses.

communicating has had an impact on everyone. Your own IQ has plummeted and will require serious rehabilitation to restore. Your husband can't understand most of what you say and doesn't really care to anymore anyway. And your baby is adopting Dr. Seuss speech patterns that will ultimately limit his career to that of greeting card writer.

On top of all this, you've begun to incessantly refer to yourself in the third person. "Mommy wants Benjamin to give her the porcelain vase." "Mommy doesn't like it when Abby punches her in the face." You're not the friggin' Queen of England. Please stick with first person and teach your child how most of the population converses. "I" think they will be better communicators, and "you" will sound like less of an a-hole.

One last thing to keep in mind regarding language is that when dealing with children, it's a huge mistake to end each statement with a question. "You need to clean up this mess and get ready for bed, *okay?*" Children are sneaky little loophole hunters. If you leave even a tiny crack in your instructions, they will find it and flaunt it. Don't ask them if they agree with your decision to punish them. "You need to sit in your room until you're ready to stop playing WWF Smackdown in the house, *okay?*" Of course it's not okay with them. They would prefer that you just sit back and let them rule the world. And the last thing your baby needs is any more power.

Can you imagine the state of the world if it were run by people who talked like the Stay-at-Home Martyr? The universe we've come to know, trust, and treasure would be forever changed.

· The judicial system would crumble:
A solemn judge stares down over the perpetrator of a horrific murder charge. "I sentence you to life in prison with no chance of parole, *okay?*"

· The institution of marriage would unwind:
A serene preacher gazes out over a young couple at their wedding altar. "Do you, Mikey-Wikey, take Jenny-Benny to go up and down, up and down all through the town?"

· Respect for government would dwindle:
"Mommy pledges allegiance to the flag of the United States of America."

· Movie classics would be scarred:
George Bailey: "What is it you want, Mary? What do you want? You want the moon? Just say the word and I'll throw a lasso around it and pull it down. Hey. That's a pretty good idea. I'll give you the moon, Mary."

Mary: "Moon pretty. See pretty moon. Moon go poo-poo."

As you can see, it's extremely important to rebuild an adult vocabulary and carry on adult conversations in adult settings with other adults. If you're willing to admit that you can't bear the thought of another round of peek-a-boo or, heaven forbid, wa-wa-in-the-bowl, then you're ready to shake up the synapses. We wouldn't jump immediately into *The Economist* or trade *Dora the Explorer* for CNN. Face it, your brain is as jiggly as the platter of geometric Jell-O figures you made for the class party. A quick jolt into *The French Revolution* may be too much for your mushy mind to handle. Start slowly. It didn't take you a day to get this way, so pace yourself. Ease into it with a gentle game of solitaire, or try to learn a new word each day. Here are some ideas to get you thinking like a new woman.

New You Glossary

Old You	New You
curves (i.e., fat)	Curves (circuit training)
rocked all night (crying baby)	rocked all night (crying "oh baby")
My Gym	my gym
whining	wining and dining
Happy Meal (with apple, not fries)	happy hour
Volvo	vulva
Goldfish crackers	gold jewelry
Baby Einstein	Einstein's theory of relativity
thong (five-dollar flip-flop)	thong (Hanky-Panky brand)
Pampers	pamper day at the spa (you deserve it!)

There are countless reasons to start strengthening your mental fortitude. According to a good friend who recently gave up all forms of dieting and exercise in favor of cultivating her talents, *interesting people don't have to be skinny*. This is great, liberating news! After decades of starving, portioning, and denying ourselves, all we really have to do is become interesting people. The bad news is that most Stay-at-Home Martyrs are not at all interesting to non-Martyrs. Let's be honest, you make Spongebob's buddy Patrick look like a rocket scientist. You have convinced yourself that your mailman actually gives a shit about every detail of your toddler's mealtime routine.

If you show your kids that you're a multifaceted person with dreams, passions, and interests, they will grow to believe that this is how a mother should be.

You must reassess. You must dig down deep and eke out some form of curiosity. You stare blankly, "How can I be expected to make myself smarter and more interesting when I spend every ounce of energy on my kids?" We know your kids are demanding and would suck the life right out of you if you let them. But you have to stop blaming them for taking up all your time. You're the adult, and you get to choose where to give your time. Your kids deserve an attentive mother, but you deserve a life that includes space for you. If you show your kids that you're a multifaceted person with dreams, passions, and interests, they will grow to believe that this is how a mother should be.

Get a Hobby—and No, PTA and Scrapbooking Do Not Count

We know what you're thinking. "What is she talking about? I have interests. I'm a busy, creative woman. Why just this morning I cooked, I read, I brainstormed, I attended a meeting, and I applied some finishing touches to my current artistic endeavor." Come on, we all know this actually means you made a smiley-face sandwich, read a chapter out of *What to Expect the Toddler Years*, decided which Discovery toy to get baby Jimmy for Christmas, showed up for the weekly PTA meeting, and then added some stickers to the holiday section of this year's family scrapbook. These child-centered activities do not count as hobbies. There is no "I" in PTA, but there is "crap" in scrapbooking. It's essential that you find an interest that does not revolve around your children. If you're overwhelmed by the idea of actually having to develop a new skill, join a book club (aka wine drinking session), as nothing ever actually needs to be accomplished. You can collect swizzle sticks for all we care, as long as they don't have your kids' names engraved on them.

Maybe it's best to build on what you already know. You can change a diaper with one hand on a moving escalator. Why not channel that talent into learning the ancient art of origami? You've embroidered your child's full name into the back of every pair of underwear he owns. Why not start making designer pillows and sell them at local farmer's markets (and spare your teenager the embarrassment of "Stephen Marcus Johnson" every time he leans over in class)? It's entirely possible that obsessing over your offspring for so long has destroyed your ability to think as an individual. Maybe you have absolutely no idea what you like. If this is the case, there are a couple ways to uncover your hidden talents.

Go to a bookstore, but DO NOT enter the children's section, even if it's story hour and your favorite children's author is signing copies of *Cluck, Cluck, Quack, Quack*. Start at the magazine rack. Nothing is as easy as sitting quietly on a wooden bench, flipping mindlessly through magazines to the soothing sounds of instrumental Beatles. See what you gravitate toward. You may find that you can't put down *Country Gardens* or *Dog Fancy*. It doesn't matter what piques your curiosity, it just matters that you're interested in something. We know a lady who collects tiny spoons from around the world. She may have been dropped repeatedly on her head as an infant (and possibly during her adult years as well), but she LOVES it. Little spoons give her such joy that she plans vacations around them, builds frames to display them, and makes friends with other spoon-crazy people.

If actually leaving the house and your children just isn't in the stars for you, then do your research from the comfort of your couch. Channel surfing is a painless way to browse through topics. Skip right past Playhouse Disney, Nickelodeon, and any other animated channel you may come across. See what strikes your fancy. If you pause on Rachael Ray cooking up a holiday roast, maybe you're a budding culinary whiz (or just really hungry). If you can't tear yourself away from HGTV, maybe you should take up woodworking and build that custom bookshelf you've been imagining since you moved in. And if you're mesmerized by the fly-fishing channel, well, maybe you should keep flipping channels (unless there happens to be a well-stocked lake next to your daughter's ballet studio).

The important thing is to invest in yourself. A hobby is a good place to begin, but there are many ways to reawaken the sleeping intellectual giant inside you.

Go Mental

We know the sheer idea of reading takes you back to twelfth grade where you trudged painfully through *Macbeth* and other hard-to-read, dead-white-guy titles. But believe us when we tell you there is an infinite universe of things worth reading. You could be immediately transported to the foot binding of a young Chinese girl, to the insane mind of a Renaissance painter. And intellectual growth aside, there is a lot of hot sex in books. Seriously. When else are you going to get behind closed doors with a naked gladiator? Or under the covers with the heroine's gorgeous husband?

If you're more of a nonfiction reader, learn the history of Moorish architecture; that'll blow everyone's mind at the next Bunko night. Really, reading just about anything will be good for your mental fortitude.

If sex with a gladiator didn't lure you in, you may need some incentive. As a parent, you're no doubt an expert sticker reward chart maker and your kids get stars and smiley faces for doing nothing so much as spitting when they brush. So why not make a chart for yourself? When you've filled in a certain number of squares or reached a total number of points, give yourself a treat. Here's a sample idea:

STICKER REWARD CHART

Today I read ...

- Any book that includes the words "child," "parent," or "family" (0 points)

- Any magazine that compares the cellulite of B-list actors in unflattering bathing suits (½ point)

- Side of cereal box (½ point)

- Newspaper article including the words "Democrat," "Republican," or "economy" (2 points)

- Any book with footnotes, endnotes, or a bibliography (5 points)

- Any book in the Hot Mom's Club series (10 points)

- *The Stay-at-Home Martyr* (1,000 points ... hey, we make the rules)

Now that you're reading, or at least thinking about reading, we're going to suggest another idea that may send you into an absolute panic: School. We know you left that painful, cruel place and vowed never to look back. But now you're older, wiser, and too busy to care about who's eating lunch with whom (or nowadays, we guess it's who's blowing whom in the playground bathroom). You no longer bathe in Clearasil, and instead of shrinking in your seat praying you won't be called on, you just might relish the opportunity to be the annoying one who knows the answer to everything.

We know quite a few women who, after having children and spending a fair amount of time at home with them, decided that if they didn't take drastic measures and learn something other than "clean up, clean up, everybody, everywhere," they were liable to snap. School for adults is very flexible and sensitive to family and work schedules. You can enroll in online classes and get your degree with one hand while mixing a bottle with the other. There are night classes, weekend classes, holiday vacation seminars, and summer school. So if you've always wished you had finished your degree, or plan to pursue a career when the kids are a little older, maybe starting your education now is a good idea. You may never have had the ability to turn a guy green with envy back in high school, but imagine your delight when you host finals week study group and your husband walks in on you tutoring a handful of nineteen-year-old city college jocks.

Or maybe it's time to fight for a cause other than little Caroline's part in the class play. Let Caroline learn to deal with her disappointment in landing the nonspeaking part of "carrot" while you take on a bigger issue like inner-city arts or animal rights, or volunteer at an abused women's shelter. Join the statewide campaign effort and teach your kids about women's suffrage and what it means to be a citizen. The world needs caring, dedicated people to fight its causes, and your child needs to learn how to say what he wants without Mommy playing Cyrano and whispering dialogue in his ear.

If money's a major source of stress in your family life, maybe it's time to think business. There are endless ways to transform your talents into cold, hard cash. How many times have you jerry-rigged a sunshade out of a blanket and a couple of hair bands? Moms invent useful items daily (usually out of frustration with poorly thought-out products). So start brainstorming, and if you feel like it's an impossible task, imagine J.K. Rowling scribbling notes on napkins while at the park with her daughter, or the "Juicy Couture" moms who are now sorting through piles of money while you sort through piles of laundry.

If you prefer having a job that offers a solid paycheck but doesn't require great creative vision, consider a home-based business. We once knew a mom who, while her kids were in preschool, thought she'd earn a little extra cash working as a phone sex operator. As much as we admired her entrepreneurial spirit, we just couldn't imagine making the beds and emptying the diaper pail while tantalizing some desperate soul into twelve minutes of billable ecstasy. And really, the only caller the Stay-at-Home Martyr is well-equipped to handle would be Mr. I-Get-Off-When-You-Treat-Me-Like-A-Bad-Baby. "Does baby not like warm milk?" "Does it give baby runny poo-poos?" We guess if the whole infantilism thing doesn't completely weird you out, it could be considered a productive application of your work experience. Otherwise, stick to what you know and invest in your mind as much as you've invested in Junior's. To sum it up, being a mother is like being in a plane crash: You need to strap on your oxygen mask first if you're going to be of any use to your kid.

Hopefully by now you're feeling inspired. You no longer start sentences with, "I'd love to, but . . ." You're excited at the prospect of taking better care of your body, mind, and wardrobe. You've enrolled in a class and you're ready to take the next step. So put on your cutest pair of panties and get ready to say "I do" all over again.

Chapter Four

'Til Death or Martyrdom Do You Part

You may remember the famous *Twilight Zone* episode in which a man wakes up hung over one morning, barely able to remember the previous night. He turns to his sleeping wife in bed and jostles her awake. His wife, a very attractive blonde woman, wakes and turns to him and immediately screams. She has no idea who he is or what he's doing in her bed. As the episode continues, no one from his life recognizes him; not neighbors, not coworkers, not family. It's as if he never existed. At his breaking point (and while being chased by police and subsequently arrested), he jolts awake, frazzled and relieved. He turns to his sleeping wife and says, "Man, I just had the weirdest dream." His wife wakes and turns toward him, saying, "Tell me about it, dear." All he can do is stare dumbstruck at the brunette woman he clearly has never seen before in his life.

Equally dumbfounded and disoriented, many married couples with children become strangers despite their close proximity. As sweet and delectable as children are, there's no denying that parenthood and matrimonial bliss don't always peacefully co-exist. In fact, not since the introduction of Erica Kane on *All My Children* have you simultaneously loved and hated anyone so much in your life. Then again, you've probably never slept so little or gained so much weight so quickly either, unless you count freshman year when cookie dough and microbrews were dorm room staples.

When a Martyr becomes completely immersed in the world of her offspring, both she and her husband can suffer. After a long day with only the addictive lyrics of "Elmo's World" playing over and over in her head, she's desperate for adult content. Ironically, this is exactly when her husband is exhausted from work and wants to veg out in front of ESPN. And if you've ever spent the day humming, "Fruit salad, yummy, yummy," you'll also understand why she's lacking any sexual impulse. She'll "throw him a bone" from time to time when she feels enough pity, but she's never really into it. Like solemn ships passing in the night, the couple grows apart.

Most women in this predicament just assume that this is the normal state of marriage after having children and that a happy, intimate marriage will resume in eighteen years or so. (Keep in mind though that by then, your husband will be having virtual sex with his Sharper Image "pleasure-bot.") Marriages can't just sit and wait on the back burner. In order to survive, a relationship that's suffering needs to be actively cared for and nurtured. First though, it's necessary to come to terms with what's really going on.

The Family Food Chain

In the early days of your marriage, your husband stood tall with pride. He was a man with a purpose, the head of the domestic pack, the protector and provider. Still basking in the afterglow of marriage, you cooked up creative ways of enticing him in the bedroom with sexy outfits and battery-operated toys. You also cooked up creative meals in your newly registered and received All-Clad pots, and served them on your complete set of everyday dishes from Crate and Barrel including table runner and cloth napkins. You proudly affixed "Mr. & Mrs." return address labels to monogrammed thank-you cards. Framed and matted wedding photos occupied every horizontal surface in your household, and you called your *husband* (remember how weird that first sounded?) hourly, desperate for him to get home because you missed his company. You lovingly studied every curve on his face and could map every freckle on his body like the night sky.

Time passed and the novelty of wedded bliss wore off slightly. You watched as friends simmered with excitement over nursery furniture and baby registries. Instead of the hourly "I love you" calls to hubby, you e-mailed him links to ovulation calendars and lists of male fertility boosters. You were ready for the next step. And whether you threw caution to the wind one wild night or spent months tallying charts and shoving thermometers into any available orifice, you got pregnant, and the world as you and your husband knew it would never be the same.

Now instead of making him an elaborate slow-cooker stew and oat-currant bread from the Cuisinart bread maker (wow, you registered for some great stuff!), your husband had to microwave himself a hot dog and eat it in the garage since the smell made you sick. Instead of staring at each other giddy and enamored, you stared at your growing belly, mesmerized and petrified, and he stared at you, wary of making a wrong move that would cause you to puke, cry, or yell. He became a committed servant, ready to retrieve freakish cravings at all hours of the night. And while he didn't get you "hot and bothered" like he had in the early days of married life, you were still frequently hot and almost always bothered.

After the baby was born, your poor husband moved to the very bottom of the family hierarchy, now getting less attention than the dog. Truth be told, even Fido got to have sex with the throw pillow from time to time. Like you, your husband was overtired, underfed, yet somehow was still expected to maintain a regular work day, share nighttime baby feeding duties, and talk you back from the dark side of postpartum on a continual basis (but without the painkillers, gifts, or doting compliments from visitors). As your love affair with your new baby grew and consumed your every affection, your husband was left to fend for himself. All the cuddling, kissing, and adoring gazes that he had once enjoyed were now reserved for the new love of your life. As smitten as he was with this new mysterious creature, he couldn't help but feel as if he had been replaced. And the more he secretly wished he could have you back to himself, the more he felt like a big jealous a-hole.

> Being honest about your partner will give you a realistic vision of what to expect, will help you handle the day-to-day needs of family life, and will show you why it's important to let go of any impossible dreams of grandeur.

How he handles these new mixed feelings of animosity and adoration is what matters. Is he too insecure to step up to the paternal plate, or does he bite off as much as he can possibly chew?

Daddy Dearest

Soon after the arrival of the baby, new mommies begin to realize that there are different kinds of daddies in the world. It becomes apparent at the park, the pediatrician's office, and the breastfeeding support group where some husbands attend every week and ask questions concerning let-down and blistered boobies while yours just stares at the oversize hooters fantasizing about the grotto pool at the Playboy Mansion. If you want to preserve your marriage, it's helpful to recognize what kind of daddy you're dealing with. Being honest about your partner will give you a realistic vision of what to expect, will help you handle the day-to-day needs of family life, and will show you why it's important to let go of any impossible dreams of grandeur.

The Hands-off Daddy

This is the daddy who prefers to parent from a comfortable chair in front of the TV. He's all for giggles, hugs, and an animated rendition of *Brown Bear, Brown Bear,* but hand him a dirty diaper and watch his face turn the color of whatever's inside of it. He loves his children but wants a wife who understands the traditional division of labor. Like a sports announcer, he watches the kids by "broadcasting" their every move. "Honey, the baby's climbing up the stairs!" He assumes he's free from having to intervene if he states the situation clearly. "Honey, the kids are sword fighting with garden tools in the backyard!" We knew a woman whose husband declared one day that he only wanted to be responsible for the kids from the neck up. And he wasn't kidding. Luckily for them, she had a great sense of humor and relished her position as sole caregiver. While a man smoking a pipe and reading the *Wall Street Journal* might bring out your inner Lorena Bobbitt, another woman might happily accept this retro dynamic. The key is for both parents to have a clear and agreeable understanding of everyone's role.

The Desperately-Wishes-He-Could-Lactate-Too Daddy

This guy dives head first into parenting. He's devoured every piece of parenting literature available. He bonds shirtless with his new baby to promote the natural flora needed for a strong immune system. He is a La Leche promoter and can't help but offer helpful breastfeeding "latch-on" tips to women buying formula at the market. He has mastered the intricacies of the Baby Bjorn and thinks a family that sleeps together grows together. While some women might fantasize about having a mate so committed to child rearing, we assure you his double-checking, expert-referencing, and constant drive to be the best father EVER would become the bane of your existence. The scenario also risks devolving into the dreaded "Double Martyr" syndrome, wherein your quest to be uber-parents (a never-ending who's-doing-a-better-job-and-sacrificing-more-and-sleeping-less tug-of-war) begins.

The Begrudgingly-Will-Do-Whatever-You-Ask-Him Daddy

This is a tricky specimen to deal with. While he's always willing to take a wailing infant for a stroll outside the restaurant when asked, he lacks initiative and adds a dramatic sigh to each completed task. When confronted, he becomes defensive and whips out a long list of things he's done for you lately. More than likely he is seriously overwhelmed. Whether it's work stress, financial worries, or the fear of his newfound role as provider, this daddy isn't coping well. He can't verbalize what he needs and more than likely doesn't even know. Try to get him to open up; give him permission to be tired, to complain. And force him to go out and take a little time to himself. Then see if the heavy sighs subside. If the loving, sensitive approach doesn't snap him out of it, ask your Begrudgingly-Will-Do-Whatever-You-Ask-Him Daddy to go begrudgingly make up his new bed on the sofa.

The Bad-Influence Daddy

This is the daddy whose inner "Dennis the Menace" drives him to feed the baby chocolate and run with the stroller like an Indy 500 racecar driver. And while the baby may squeal in delight when weaving at high speeds through crowded malls and bounce like a monkey at the sight of a Hershey bar, you're left gasping and frowning at every turn. You chastise your Bad-Influence Daddy for playing Tower of Terror with your one-year-old and want to kill him when you find them eating popcorn and watching *Indiana Jones and the Temple of Doom*. (Who the hell doesn't know popcorn is among the top five chokeable foods for young children?!) But the truth is, you married a bad boy. You chose him (and more than likely squealed too when he drove home from your date like an Indy 500 racer). So the next time he forgets to buckle the baby properly in the car seat, smack him and then smack yourself for thinking Evel Knievel could ever become Mr. Mom.

Depending on the kind of daddy you're dealing with, your level of frustration will vary. Whether he's helpful or detached, overprotective or a risk taker, developing a partnership while learning to care for a child is an enormous challenge. The only one whose needs really get met when baby arrives is baby. But once that initial newborn survival period passes, effort must be made to remember each other. It sounds simple, but it's not an easy thing to do. If you've spent months (or years) obsessing over nap routines and kid-friendly meals, you may simply have no recollection of what makes a marriage thrive. And, more specifically, what makes a man happy.

We Know What Boys Like

If the idea of taking care of hubby conjures up images of a hot bowl of SpaghettiO's, Goldfish crackers, and a Juicy Juice box, it's time to reacquaint yourself with the male species. Men may not be the complex creatures that women are, but they do have one or two needs beyond a thick steak and a hand job. Since we have erred on the side of ignoring our mates, we have invited our darling husbands to watch over our shoulders and contribute to this section, provided they are able to sit for an extended period of time without burping, expelling gas, or using bathroom humor. We figured having a man's insight would add a level of . . . Oh crap, never mind, they're outta here. But they did make it a whole forty-eight seconds.

Anyway, there are some basic things you should remember when sharing your life with a man. Men want to feel like capable, strong, and valuable assets whom you could not live without. While in reality you may be able to turn palm frond condensation into drinking water and slay a wild boar for meat (and your husband has trouble unloading the dishwasher—really, how friggin' hard is it to remember where the wine glasses go?), he still needs to believe he's the man and that

> Men want to feel like capable, strong, and valuable assets whom you could not live without.

you desperately need him. Here are some simple ways to make a man feel like a man and conjure up your knight in shining armor.

· Despite your ability to construct a solar-powered K'nex Ferris Wheel while making the beds and dinner, feign complete ignorance when hooking up the new DVD player and make your man feel like a techno star.

· Squeal when you come across any indoor insect larger than a Tic Tac, and if you're feeling especially dramatic, climb on top of a chair until he comes to the rescue and rids the household of said predator.

• Ask for help when moving heavy objects. We all know that after years of carrying a fifty-pound toddler in one hand and a ten-pound grocery bag in the other, you could lift a car to retrieve a lost tennis ball if needed. But as far as hubby is concerned, you're a demure, fragile little flower who relies on his manly physique and intimidating determination to get the job done.

As we've discussed in the previous chapters, men want companions who inspire them to improve themselves. You can't expect a man to develop rock-hard abs and better communication skills if his wife smells like Desitin and rolls her eyes at his every attempt to be handy around the house.

As most of you well know from seeing your spouse gawk at any female in tight pants, men are visual. While you may prefer mood lighting and a warm cozy feeling, men want to see the raw, graphic nature of things. They're excited and intrigued by beauty and mystery and, of course, nudity of any kind. Beyond wanting to sneak a peek of you all soaped up in the shower, men want to have sex. They're happier, less stressed, and more eager to please you if they're getting action on a semi-regular basis. (The specifics of getting naked and having relations after children will be further discussed in the next chapter.) A woman can't give her man what he needs if she greets him after a long day with a barrage of:

"You're tired?! You should try to handle my life for a day!"

"You never talk to me anymore."

"Do you think *you* could plan dinner once in a while?"

"How can you expect me to be in the mood after an entire day of kids hanging on me like a jungle gym?"

As tired as you are after a day of dealing with kids, your man needs time to unwind, too (and accompanying little Avery to Brownie Campfire Sing-a-Long doesn't count). Let him go out one night a week to play tennis or meet an old (male) friend for a drink. Even if it's just fifteen minutes of putzing around the house without being handed a "honey-do" list, it will make him a happier husband and a more attentive daddy.

Clearly, not every man is worthy of adoration. Some men just don't have the self-esteem, motivation, or grooming habits to make a woman swoon. Sometimes the blame game has gone on for so long that no one is willing to reverse the negativity and be the first to start over. "Why should I be all loving when he's a lazy piece that does nothing to help me?" "How can I possibly adore her when she criticizes every single thing I do? I don't hold the baby right. I give the baby a bath all wrong. Hell, I even make a noise when I chew." The bottom line is someone's gotta give. For the sake of your happiness, your children's mental health, and keeping your family free of custody arrangements, start liking each other a little more every day. Try to remember what you once loved about him. And if it means that you have to bite your tongue when he chugs your toddler's apple juice directly from the container, so be it. If you have to

> For the sake of your happiness, your children's mental health, and keeping your family free of custody arrangements, start liking each other a little more every day.

turn away when he dresses your precious little darling in plaid shorts and a polka-dot top, then turn. And if you have to count to ten to avoid snapping when you find an hours-old poop in your baby's diaper and he claims "she must have just done it," go ahead and count to twenty so you don't hurl the petrified poop in his face. There are worse things in the world that have been forgiven. Everyone is flawed and everyone deserves love.

Once you've thought about what your husband needs and wants, and have hopefully begun repairing the rift, it's time to focus on what a family needs to be functional.

It's a Family Affair

There exists a simple, successful, age-old structure where a mother and father operate as the center of the family. Children bounce and flail around the perimeter of this rock-solid core, and this is what gives them the opportunity to test boundaries, learn from their mistakes, and grow into halfway decent adults. In the past decade or so, some brainiac decided to reorganize the model and promote children to the center position. Whoever decided that children in power was a good idea clearly never read *Lord of the Flies*. If they'd have studied these dynamics at all, they would have realized that with age comes wisdom, and with youth comes chaos, selfishness, and low-rider baggy jeans that show off way too much butt crack.

Don't make your children responsible for their own upbringing. It's understandable that you want your child to be happy and adore you, and that you're willing to go to great lengths to ensure that he never feels pain. But it's also important to keep in mind that when little Evan sobs, "If you loved me, you would buy me a Thomas the Tank Engine roundhouse!" what he really means is, "Please be the adult and teach me that I can't go ballistic when life doesn't give me exactly what I want." I'm not suggesting that you say no all the time or that you cut off all lines of communication, simply that you mean what you say, and that you make sure your child knows Mommy and Daddy are a unified front who handle the decision making and cannot be divided.

Just like your baby glances back at you frequently when learning to crawl away, your older child needs to know that you're always there, ready to intervene and help him learn how to function safely and successfully in the world (or as the Bad-Influence Daddy would so eloquently put it, "knock him into next week"). Reclaiming your role as center of your family won't be easy. It will require you to change how you approach your life in general. Instead of seeing the world through what's-best-for-baby-colored glasses, you will need to start thinking in terms of what's best for family.

This means that if you and your husband have finally sat down at the end of the day together on the couch and little Marisa desperately wants to take flying leaps onto Daddy a la Jay Jay the Jet Plane, just say no. Don't let her hurl herself repeatedly into the middle of your moment. Don't even sugarcoat it or negotiate the terms (she will win and get at least five more jumps in before retiring to an effective pout). Say no and mean it. At first she'll be upset, but through her teary dramatics she'll witness a couple that values their relationship and time together. As much as she claims to hate you for not paying attention to her, she'll feel safer knowing Mommy and Daddy love each other and will grow up with a healthy understanding on which to build her own relationships.

This same attitude applies in most circumstances— to adult parties, dinners, conversations, and decision making. It's absolutely reasonable to expect children to behave respectfully, go to bed earlier than you, and to eat (or at least gag down one bite of) what is being served for dinner. You and your spouse are the glue that holds the family together. It's crucial that you learn to operate as a team and—brace yourself, dear Stay-at-Home Martyr—this may mean it's time to make some changes.

What to Expect When You're Expecting Too Much

The Stay-at-Home Martyr is notorious for her sky-high expectations. As much as she claims to want her husband to take on some of her load, she can't stand to let him do things his way and can't help but correct him at every interaction. "Don't you know we fold the towels in thirds, not in halves?" "Can't you ever remember to use the heated wipes?" Sound familiar? Plus, having someone there who actually helps out makes it difficult for a Martyr to really revel in being so put-upon. Pushing your mate away from "the team" may make you think you're ready to join Joan of Arc as one of history's great martyrs, but it makes the already strained marital situation worse. This leads to resentment on both sides—a woman who feels overwhelmed and abandoned, and a man who feels like a belittled and insignificant other.

These feelings may date back to pregnancy when you stewed over the fact that *The Birth Partner* sat for nine months untouched on your husband's nightstand. You knew the exact day and time of conception while he couldn't even remember the due date. You knew the process of fetal cell division and the day your fetus took his first pee in your amniotic fluid while he couldn't tell you the difference between Braxton Hicks and Taylor Hicks. And things haven't improved much since then. While you've memorized every sleep-related book on the shelf, your husband thinks Ferber is that guy who makes little jars of baby food.

You may be wondering how on Earth you'll ever develop a solid partnership under these less-than-satisfactory circumstances. The bottom line, Ms. Martyr, is that you need to lower your soaring expectations. That's not to say you can't strive to be good at what you do. And you'll undoubtedly and understandably hate your mate on occasion. But you must let him develop his own relationship with the kids and do things his own way. This remains true even if his way isn't the most efficient, cost-effective, or expert-approved approach. Your kids don't care if he puts their pants on backwards. And if he forgets to bring spare diapers and wipes to the mall, I guarantee next time he ventures out with baby he'll remember.

Everyone knows the key to a successful group project is teamwork. A strong team grows out of good communication.

And we all know how difficult it is to keep communicating when there are towels to tri-fold and wipes to warm, and an endless stream of household functions that must be done your way.

Communication Is the Key to Boredom

The marital communication problem is twofold. First, there's a serious lack of content. Whether it's that "hilarious" story about the time in college your husband ran through the dorm cafeteria in nothing but his socks and ski mask, or that same inappropriate joke he seems to save for meeting new and important people, you've heard it all before. And truth be told, he's heard all your stuff before, too. Really, how many stories do each of us actually have to tell? Our inner libraries are limited to our experience. And most of the parents we know aren't off machete-hacking their way through lush jungles or studying the mating habits of giant pandas in the wild. It's especially difficult to gather any colorful life experience when you're responsible for small people on a minute-to-minute basis. Seriously, how much friggin' material is there between the pantry and the Diaper Genie? Who can bring an audience to the edge of their seats with a riveting tale of poorly organized music classes or the outrageous cost of a third-grade field trip? The world of the stay-at-home mom just doesn't have that much to offer. So by the time your husband walks through the door at the

end of the day, you're so desperate for anything remotely adult that you'll squeeze every last drop of information out of him.

"Did you talk to Rick about vacation time?"

"I mentioned it, but we only had a few minutes before the meeting."

"What did he say?"

"He said he'd get back to me."

"And what did you say?"

"I said . . . okay."

"And then what did he say?"

"He sort of nodded and then walked off."

"Walked off like he was mad? Or walked off like 'no big deal'?"

"Just kind of walked off."

"Oh my god, like he was annoyed? Or ignoring you? What if he's mad? Maybe you shouldn't have said anything."

"You've been bugging me for weeks to ask him."

This can continue indefinitely, or until the guy finally flatly refuses to relay any more information about the outside world. This leads to the notorious "quiet husband" syndrome. You may have no idea why your husband isn't excited to share things with you. All you know is that it bothers you to no end. Lay your resentment aside and put yourself in his shoes for a moment. Try to remember how it felt when you were little and your mom had to know every detail about your school day. School sucked enough without having to relive it just minutes after it ended each day. Let him talk to you about what matters to him. If you took Chapter Three to heart and cultivated some form of hobby or interest, and are pumping iron with your newly energized brain cells, you should have plenty to talk about. It's understandable that women become resentful of their husbands who get to "live it up" at the office by talking uninterrupted on the phone and going out to lunch at a place that doesn't offer crayons, while Mommy is stuck at home eating cold Delimex taquitos. But the job of motherhood is not limited to a mundane existence. It's up to both people to bring new and interesting tales back to the relationship. You simply cannot be a parasite that feeds off your husband for mental stimulation. It puts too much pressure on him, and it does nothing to promote your own self-growth, interests, or rapidly deteriorating mental capacity.

> You cannot be a parasite that feeds off your husband for mental stimulation. It puts too much pressure on him, and it does nothing to promote your own self-growth, interests, or rapidly deteriorating mental capacity.

It's Not What You Say, It's How Evil You Say It

Beyond needing to improve *what* you talk about, it's important to keep in mind *how* you talk to each other. It's way too easy to be nasty and insensitive when you're sleep-deprived and resentful. Words like "always," "never," and "worthless piece of crap" seem to just roll off your tongue with incredible ease. Some simple, therapist-approved ways to communicate better are starting sentences with "I" instead of "you" and avoiding superlatives when possible. Instead of "You never do a damn thing to help around this house, so clear your calendar, buddy, 'cuz you've got an appointment with Mr. Hoover and Mr. Clean!," try a more tempered "I feel like I'm doing most of the cleaning lately. Do you think maybe on Sunday we could work together to get caught up?"

We can't stress enough how important it is to learn how to talk to your spouse. Speak from your own perspective ("I feel like . . ."), stay on topic (no snowballing), avoid name calling and finger pointing, and if you don't see a quick resolve for the spat, wait until your kids go to sleep. Fighting in front of your kids scares them more than the most feared boogeyman or loud public bathroom toilet flush. And finally, for god's sake, get a sense of humor. We're all going to have our moments of conflict, and if we can learn to laugh at ourselves, we'll spend a good portion of our lives a lot less miserable.

When our friend Lorie's second baby was born, she and her husband were wrestling with the "how to get the baby to sleep for more than twelve minutes at a time" thing. They decided that the reason their other child (and dog) hadn't slept through the night in seven solid years was because they had failed to create a predictable bedtime routine. So this time they committed. They bathed the baby with lavender oil, played soothing tribal sounds from around the world, dimmed the lights, fed him, swaddled him, then laid him down in the baby wedge thing everyone claimed was the magic ingredient in getting an infant to sleep. They then made a pact and swore that they'd get this baby to learn to fall asleep on his own (i.e., "cry it out"). And under no circumstances would they cave. (To you new parents this may sound harsh, but to those of you who haven't had the luxury of REM sleep since preconception, you know what

we're sayin'.) They retreated to the
kitchen and proceeded to listen as
he howled like no other eight-week-
old creature on Earth could possibly do.
Nothing can rattle the nervous system like
a wailing infant. Seconds felt like minutes,
minutes became centuries. Her husband was
sure the swaddle had unraveled (despite the Velcro
and origami folding it required). He was convinced
the poor little bugger was suffocating, or overheated, or
still hungry, or lonely. She stood her ground (remembering
all too well the seven years of rocking and nursing and
coercing she did for her first child). He said he had to go
peek and make sure everything was okay. Just peek. He
reemerged soon after, carrying a bright red screaming little
baby burrito and undoing all that they had agreed upon. She
was fuming and snapped.

"What in the world are you doing?!"

He was equally pissed at her for questioning his
decision. "Oh, I don't know. Maybe trying to get him to stop
crying."

"He's crying because he's tired and you just ruined the
whole stinking bedtime routine by bringing him into the
bright kitchen."

He looked at her with daggers. "He's crying because
he's hungry."

"He just ate for an hour straight. He's not hungry." She
was boiling like a pressure cooker, ready to blow.

"Well, he just slept for two hours straight before that.
Maybe he's *not* tired." She just stared at him, festering
with postpartum disdain. He continued. "And since you're

clearly the expert here, why don't *you* tell me why he's been crying for forty-two minutes straight?"

"Maybe he's crying because *he* thinks you're an asshole, too."

She froze, stunned that such horrific words had actually come out of her mouth. He froze too. Even the baby froze. They stared at each other for a good fifteen seconds, unfamiliar with this level of offense, and then broke down in uncontrollable belly laughter, something they hadn't done since trying to make the parts fit during third-trimester sex. This began a new approach to handling stress in their relationship. Now that the baby is learning to talk, they save the profanity for special private moments but have learned to diffuse intense moments by being irreverent. They rarely get their feathers ruffled and frequently find themselves laughing when others would be crying.

Perhaps not everyone can solve their marital disdain quite so easily. But there's no doubt that things are never as dire as they seem in the heat of the moment. And laughing is a great way to bridge the gap between contempt and contemplating divorce.

How to Start a Fire with Wet Wood

Now that you recognize the situation and have been reminded what makes a strong marriage and a content mate, you may be wondering how in the world to implement all this abstract information. You know your husband wants to be adored and respected and all that, but it still bugs the hell out of you when he plops down on the couch and watches *Family Guy* while the kids are starving, the dog needs to go out, and the phone is ringing incessantly. It's one thing to *want* a happy marriage, but how on Earth does a frazzled, tired Stay-at-Home Martyr reignite a flame that burned out long ago? Here are some simple ideas for approaching your marriage in a healthier, more forgiving, and less-likely-to-push-him-off-a-cliff-and-make-it-look-like-an-accident kind of way.

The Thirty-Day Rule

Like most women, we have memories like stainless steel traps when it comes to mistakes. We can access annoying things our husbands said or did years ago with splendid detail and frightening accuracy. Men aren't naturally like us, yet some hapless husbands have the nerve to claim they never forget important events. Within seconds, an angry wife's got him pinned on his back and sweating under an assault of "missed dinners," "Valentine's Day," "second anniversary," "great-aunt's seventieth birthday gift" he failed to pick up, and "two prenatal Lamaze classes" he failed to attend. If he resists her imminent victory and tries to further defend himself, she goes for the knockout with a can't-lose, "And most men don't forget their wedding vows while standing at the altar of their own wedding!"

It's way too easy to rely on this well-stocked arsenal in heated moments. And regardless of how good it feels to be right, it's really not fair and doesn't help strengthen the bond. Everyone makes mistakes. Everyone says things without thinking and wishes they could take them back. When problems come up, it's far healthier and generally nicer to focus on the future instead of rehashing the past (although it's not nearly as rewarding).

> Having a limited amount of time to throw something in your spouse's face redefines the way you communicate, increases your ability to forgive, and helps to preserve the future of your relationship.

That's why it may be helpful to implement the "Thirty-Day Rule." If your husband fails to remember the parent-teacher conference or forgets to pay the electric bill and you wind up reading Eric Carle by candlelight while your freezer full of homemade baby food cubes thaw, you only have thirty days to hold it against him. If you "accidentally" break his favorite boot-shaped beer mug or fail to send a thank-you card to his mother for the lovely hand-crocheted holiday wall hanging she sent and no doubt expects to enjoy while visiting, he can only bring it up for those thirty short days.

Having a limited amount of time to throw something in your spouse's face redefines the way you communicate, increases your ability to forgive, and helps to preserve the future of your relationship. And reminding your husband that he only has two days left to ridicule you for forgetting the dog at the vet can turn a sour situation much sweeter.

We feel we must add that in a situation of extreme stupidity, a waiver may be granted. At times there are actions so severe that they permeate into the deepest bowels of your long-term memory and have no expiration date. Examples include trying to remove tree sap from the car hood with nail polish remover and not realizing the error of your ways until it's much too late. Or, after being told time and time again of the dangers involved, insisting on leaving the baby alone on top of the changing room table only to realize the warnings were valid. Or our personal favorite, when a friend woke her husband to tell him that she just took a pregnancy test and it was positive, he simply uttered, "That's great, honey," and rolled over and went back to sleep. These are the types of actions that a woman never forgets. Maybe forgives. Maybe looks back on and laughs. But never forgets.

One Nice Thing: A Real Life Fairy Tale

One afternoon two friends, were sitting at the park trying to catch up between swing pushes, retrieving stolen toys, and cleaning sand out of their toddlers' mouths. Mid-thought Melissa stopped and gazed at Holly as if she had been struck over the head with a mallet.

"You know what? I'm pretty sure I'm a terrible bitch of a wife."

Holly laughed because Melissa was always this straightforward and self-deprecating, and she loved her friend for it. She tried to respond optimistically:

"Oh, come on, we all have days when we're not very nice." She thought for a moment, gave her wailing two-year-old a push on the swing.

"No, I'm pretty much always a bitch. I'm critical. I'm not complimentary. I love to remind him what he's not doing for me. And I never do anything nice for him." Melissa stared at her friend, hoping she would reassure her in some way.

"Wow, you *are* a bitch." Melissa's face fell. "But now that I think about it, I'm kind of a bitch too."

From that moment on, they agreed to do "one nice thing" each day for their husbands. Not make-a-mushy-collage or why-I-love-you poems, but simple nice things. Rub his shoulders while he sits on his ass and does nothing. Be loving even when he has the nerve to ask when dinner will be ready after you walk in the door from seven hours of carpooling between two schools, the tutor, gymnastics, soccer, the grocery store, and the groomer to pick up the dog (who, by the way, gets to the salon WAY more often than you do). Their hope was that this good-karma-producing nicey-niceness would spread and before they knew it their whole family would be tripping over each other being loving. They thought their plan was brilliant! They would fight marital strife by being nice wives. They would rewire the circuitry and learn to love their husbands all over again.

They spoke after a couple days, "Have you been doing your nice things?" Melissa reflected a minute.

"Does not yelling at him for forgetting it was trash day count?"

"Absolutely!" Holly confirmed.

"Okay, then yes. What about you?"

"Well, the first two days I forgot, so today I'm going to do three nice things. Actually, make it four because I turned him down in bed last night."

"Good idea."

Since then they've done many nice things for their

husbands, and their husbands in turn have done nice things for them, including entering a pact to take turns rubbing each other's feet once a week (despite the fact that the women deserve extra points for touching their husbands' dried-out heels and uncut toenails that rival any found in *Guinness Book of World Records)*. It's a long road to the kindness they bestowed upon each other when they were first married, but perhaps this is as good as it's going to get for a while.

We all know in our hearts that our husbands deserve nicer, loving wives who can find the silver lining on a cloud of smelly, soiled laundry, and we should strive to be those women. One nice thing a day may not put us up there with Mother Teresa or Angelina Jolie, but it's a damn good place to start.

Keeping the Upper Hand

Marriage experts may disagree, but we know more than a couple women who swear they have healthy marriages because they have managed to keep the upper hand. These are not manipulative, shallow women, but rather women who claim they've uncovered the true nature of what men want. And simply put, they want what is not easily attained or understood. A Stay-at-Home Martyr who has completely given herself up is not something worth coveting. What man desires the affection of a woman who is needy and insecure? What man lusts after a lady in a "cow jumping over the moon" bathrobe?

I'm sure you're wondering what these insightful women do to keep themselves on top. They preserve an air of mystery. They have plans. They walk with a certain "wouldn't you like to know" attitude. Of course they are mothers too, so the air of mystery might just be about them contemplating what to make for dinner. The plans may be an exciting trip to the supermarket. And the "wouldn't you like to know" attitude may be the result of a thong underwear wedgie they are trying out after reading Chapter Two. What it all boils down to is self-esteem. The details don't matter as much as the attitude. If a woman believes she can turn the heads of men and attract savvy, intelligent friends, the world will respond accordingly. And if she confidently and playfully addresses her husband instead of muttering and generally ignoring him, watch his interest and affection rise (among other things).

Counseling before Canceling

What if you've tried everything and it still doesn't change things? You've tried seeing things from his perspective. You've been nicer and more loving. And still your marriage isn't working. If you're considering throwing in the burp cloth and calling it a day, please exhaust all possibilities before deciding on divorce. If there is even a shred of respect left between you and your spouse, there is hope. And if the vow you took before God, Allah, or that Internet-ordained minister at the drive-thru chapel in Vegas isn't enough to make you think twice, consider having to watch your children drive away with your husband and his new undereducated, oversexed girlfriend on Wednesdays, Saturdays, and every other Thanksgiving.

Let's face it, though, not every problem can be solved and sometimes a Martyr really is a victim. As important as we believe it is to be loyal and committed to your marriage, there are a few things that a woman should never have to tolerate. If your spouse is abusive (either physically or mentally), it's time to pack up the exersaucer and run. If he hits you, your kids, or the liquor cabinet too often, you must get out. It's your job (no matter how scary it is) to protect your children.

Another acceptable reason to bail out is if he's caught cheating. With cheating normally comes lying (among other things like chlamydia and half-siblings for your children). Some people are capable of forgiving their spouse for adultery. And we suppose in some cases, it really did only happen "one time," it didn't mean anything, they really are sorry, and they won't ever talk to that cheesy-skank-of-a-cocktail-waitress again. It's our belief, though, that people who lie generally continue to lie, and that a relationship without trust is one that won't withstand the test of time.

Unless you're dealing with one of these major problems, it's best to just let the little things go. And while a little thing (like his "little thing") can seem like a monumental deficiency (and leave you sighing longingly at the salami counter of the local Italian market), it really isn't grounds for divorce. When life gives you lemons, make lemon drop martinis. And when your husband makes you crazy, make it a double.

Chapter Five

From Dog Tired to Doggy Style

Now that you've taken the necessary steps to rebuild your crumbling relationship, don't be surprised if your husband starts looking at you again with that old gleam in his eye. And this time, the gleam's not caused by another bout of pinkeye your kid brought home from preschool. He may even feel more confident to make a move on you, something he's been too afraid to do in the past for fear of being rejected. Yes, now that the foundation of your relationship is getting stronger, your husband's excited to think that, to ease his sexual frustration, he may not have to take matters in his own hand anymore.

Contrary to how he's feeling, you may not be all too thrilled at the idea. True, you're happy that the two of you have been laughing more and holding hands from time to time, but that doesn't mean that you're eager to climb into bed again and bump uglies. Far from it. You may not have those same urges and are completely exhausted at the end of the day. In fact, you haven't been this afraid of having sex since the time you first laid eyes on male genitalia.

Whether you like it or not, it seems that making love is something that's in your near future. But unlike the old days when you had sex simply to mark another thing off your to-do list, there is the possibility that you may actually like it again. On that note, here are some tricks to put the love back in lovemaking and putting some heat back in those dying embers. Let's put a garter on the Martyr and get down to business!

You Know Your Sex Life Is Suffering When . . .

- You find yourself making a mental list of private school options during sex.

- Your husband tells you to pack your bag for a weekend getaway and you start piling Huggies Overnights in the diaper bag.

- You're at an elegant dinner party with your husband and you lean over to cut his meat mid-conversation.

- You find yourself fantasizing about straddling the pommel horse for your child's gymnastics coach.

- You and your mommy friends get in a heated debate over which of the Wiggles would be the better lover.

The demise of a marital sex life is often a blur. One minute you're coochy-cooing your way down Lover's Lane and the next minute you're dividing up assets and playing hardball over visitation rights. Keeping your sex drive alive once you have kids takes a lot of work, and sometimes a few toys. The important thing to remember is that you can't let it die! Once you give up and become one of those couples who never has sex, you're just a hop, skip, and a jump away from being a guest on those very special "uncensored" episodes of Dr. Phil (and you know some old boyfriend will be watching and thinking that dumping your ass was the best decision he ever made). So how do you breathe life into your dying sex life? Read on.

My-Husband-Makes-Me-So-Mad-Libs

We know what you're thinking. How can you possibly switch gears so easily and go from a "bitter-resentful-wife-who-thinks-her-husband-is-a-worthless-piece-of-doo-hickey" to a "sex-craved-temptress-who'll-drive-her-man-wild"? A change so severe would entail a stiff shot of Baileys, a dozen raw oysters, and that erotic Sting song that always manages to get you in the mood. And even more importantly, it would entail letting go of your anger. Yes, the only way that you can truly go from being a Mad Martyr to a Mad-for-You-Martyr is to release the resentment and frustration you've been harboring for so long.

   To do this, try playing a round of My-Husband-Makes-Me-So-Mad-Libs. It's just like the version you used to play as a kid, only much more vindictive and fun! Here's how it works: Think of your man, and write down the first eight adjectives that come to mind to describe him (remember, an adjective describes something . . . in this case examples include

"asinine," "moronic," or "big ol' lump of lard"). Go ahead
. . . we'll wait.

1. _____
2. _____
3. _____
4. _____
5. _____
6. _____
7. _____
8. _____

Great. Now, insert those adjectives into the following
story:

"Last week, my _____ husband did something
typical. Thinking it would please me enough to get me
into bed with him, he actually tried to do laundry. Being
as _____ as he is, he had no idea that you're
supposed to separate the whites from the colors, or he was
just too _____ to actually do it. Also, he was
too _____ to know that not everything should
go into a hot dryer. Because he's such a _____,
I now have a drawer full of gray underwear and my
daughter has a new selection of European cashmere
sweaters to use on her baby dolls. How could I have
married such a _____, _____, and
_____-ass man!"

There! Feel better? We knew you would. You've gotten
rid of some of your anger and resentment, and you're able

to stare at your man with loving eyes (just don't look down or your tattered, dry-clean-only silk blouse will bring back all your rage). Now that your spirit has been renewed, you're ready to take the next step.

Date Night

Unlike your husband who can get turned on watching you pick up dirty clothes from the floor, you need a bit more help. Women aren't visual like men, and we need to connect on a deeper, emotional level. That's why it's vital that if you and your mate haven't mated in a while, you need to spend time together as a couple. Without your child around to distract you, you can sit down to a meal and actually speak in complete sentences, chew your food, and have dessert all to yourself without having to share it with your kid. The mood is romantic, the lighting is dim, and you'll be able to nurture your relationship and see your husband as someone more than "that guy I used to know."

The mood is romantic, the lighting is dim, and you'll be able to nurture your relationship and see your husband as someone more than "that guy I used to know."

Of course, none of that can happen if you're sitting at a restaurant worrying that the fruit of your loins is home and in some type of peril. Or if you're constantly calling the babysitter to make sure everything's all right. Maybe a night on the town is such an unfathomable idea that you're considering skipping ahead to the next chapter. But remember, the best thing you can do for your child is keep your relationship with your mate healthy.

If you think you're ready to dip your toe in the uncharted waters of "date night," start brainstorming some things you can do as a couple. It might not be easy at first. You can effortlessly design a social calendar for your child that includes theater productions, athletic events, social outings, and book signings, but you seem to draw a blank when your husband asks you where you'd like to have dinner. Get creative. Plan activities that support interaction. As great as it would be to catch the new Brad Pitt shirtless movie, you will return home that night having only spoken to your husband when you asked him to pass the popcorn. Once you've accepted the fact that you aren't allocating enough time to your marriage, it's time to bring down the roadblocks that are keeping you from leaving the house.

Hiring a Sitter

We're sure your number one excuse for a dismal social calendar is lack of child care. How many times have you sighed and declared, "I really wish I could be at your party, but we just don't have a reliable sitter"? What the Stay-at-Home Martyr really means when she says this is, "There's no way I'm leaving the person I live and breathe for with some teenage girl obsessively texting her BFF while my child decides to play dolphin trainer in the pool." And we hear you. There's nothing more dreadful than peeling a child whose wailing, "Don't leave me, Mommy!" off your leg so that you can go out and enjoy a mediocre movie (that you could watch on DVD) and eat a meal (that you could prepare faster and cheaper at home). It's in that heart-wrenching moment of departure that you must remember all that we've discussed. Make it your mantra: "I deserve a life. My husband deserves a wife. I deserve a life. My husband deserves a wife." Repeat while peeling said child from extremities. We guarantee that once you're out of earshot, your child will be gleefully skipping around the yard playing pony lessons with the sitter. The tears and torture are reserved exclusively for you, so the less you indulge them by hanging around and comforting your little Scarlett O'Horror, the better. We know this sounds cold, but once a child understands that you're leaving regardless of her dramatic performance (and that you will always come back), she'll become more comfortable with the arrangement.

In some cases a child needs extra reassurance. Some children are so attached that they would climb back in the womb if it were physically possible. To help them deal with transitions give them some little token of yourself before you leave. They won't care if it's a nickel from your wallet, an old beaded necklace, or, in desperate times, a piece of "magic pocket string." Hopefully one of these things will help get your child through the separation, but if not, you can always resort to blackmail. Nothing says goodbye like a trip to the candy cupboard.

Once you've accepted the fact that leaving your home for brief stints of adult amusement is ultimately better for your marriage (which in turn is better for your child), you'll need some moral support and guidance in your hunt for the perfect (or generally acceptable) babysitter. There are competent, loving people out there who will take wonderful care of your children. There are also creepy people, negligent people, and people who think that it's acceptable to charge $18 an hour and watch *E! True Hollywood Story* while the kids decide to finger paint the dog. Just because someone is offering to help doesn't mean you should accept. If your mother-in-law would relish an opportunity to watch the kids for you but insists that adult-strength Tylenol is the same thing as Junior Tylenol only cheaper, and lets your toddler drink Diet Coke against your wishes, it's probably worth paying someone else to watch the kids.

Most new mothers we know have no idea where or how to track down a good babysitter. A few places you may want to avoid in your quest might be:

• the local methadone clinic

• a *Lolita* book club discussion

• the adult section of the video store

• any "_____ Anonymous" meeting

• a local Swedish modeling agency talent fair

Here are some places where you might have better luck.

Mommy-N-Me Teacher/Preschool Aide

This pool of professionals is a veritable gold mine of underpaid, overqualified, baby-crazy educators. They are frequently studying for better underpaid jobs as teachers or child-care administrators. Despite their high educational level, they are for some reason still willing to sing "Tuna Fish" at the top of their lungs and have memorized recipes for Ooblick, Gak, and Play-Doh.

College Child Development Department

Along the same lines as the preschool pool, your local college or junior college child development department is brimming with starving students, eager to implement their newfound understanding of Piaget's developmental stages (and equally eager to make rent this month).

Babysitting Co-op

If every penny you earn has been allocated to the diaper, milk, and Robeez fund and you simply can't scrounge together enough for a night out, consider spearheading a babysitting co-op. The way this works is a group of frugal, struggling, or granola-y parents agree to trade babysitting duty so that everyone gets a night out once a month. These can be moms from your play group, breastfeeding support group, preschool, soccer team, etc. The key to making this potentially volatile arrangement work (for you) is to make sure the most capable couple in the group gets your kids on your night out, and that you wind up with the most docile ones on your night of duty. (Avoid the biters, screechers, and pet smackers if possible.)

Agency or Referral Service

If you have a history of bad judgment when it comes to hiring, dating, and setting people up, you may want to employ a reputable agency in your hunt for a child-care provider. They will charge you a fee, but their screening process entails more than "a good vibe" and will offer you reassurance that your sitter isn't hiding an outstanding warrant, a lead foot, suspended license, abuse charges, or mafia connections.

The Misunderstood "Manny"

What first comes to mind when you see a man-nanny or "manny" caring for someone's young children? People automatically assume he must be gay (not that there's anything wrong with that) or have a living room frighteningly full of irresistible arcade games and toys. This myth must be dispelled. Sometimes a male caregiver is exactly what you need. Are you raising unruly boys with a husband who travels or works late far too often? Are you negotiating a

divorce and wishing there was a man around for your kids to spend time with? Or maybe your jock husband is coaching his way through fatherhood while your artistic son would love nothing more than a manny to sit and build elaborate medieval models with him. While the word "babysitter" may not conjure up images of a deep voice and facial hair, it can certainly be a possibility worth exploring.

Borrowing Babysitters

Obviously it would be lovely if you could just borrow a sitter who had been tried and tested on someone else's kids. This is a great resource if a) your friend is okay with farming out such a precious asset (always assure them that they will retain first rights). Or b) your friendship with her is less important than having a good babysitter on hand. Keep in mind, though, that nanny-poaching is a crime punishable by exclusion from birthday parties, purse parties, and family barbecues.

Depending on your level of discomfort, you will need to equip yourself with some form of sitter surveillance. This can be as simple as a cell phone and a nosy neighbor who's willing to pop in, or as elaborate as a hidden "teddy bear" nanny-cam to keep you informed of the wonderful, creative, and developmentally appropriate things happening in your home.

Once you've found a suitable person and have wired your house like a CIA operative, it's time to actually gather your things and leave the house. The first time you may only be capable of circling the block twenty times and then returning, positive that Gretchen the preschool teacher is plotting to sell your baby in an international porn ring. The key is not to give up. The next time Gretchen comes over (assuming she'll come back after catching you digging through her purse for syringes and the porn ring contact info), circle the block twenty-one times. Then twenty-two. And when you start to feel braver, test your limits with a trip to the market. Keep upping your ability to venture out and before you know it you'll be bar dancing in Vegas for the weekend wondering whose kids keep calling you.

But I Don't Wanna!

You've finished your delicious date night dinner, you've polished off a bottle of decent wine, your babysitter's gone home, and as you head up the stairs toward the bedroom, the awful realization hits you: There's a good chance you're gonna have to have sex tonight. While technically after having children you're "postpartum" for the rest of your life, you can really only use that excuse to avoid sex for about six weeks (longer if your husband never read those baby books you gave him, and whose ever does?). I know you can't even fathom someone else touching your already overworked breasts, and the mere idea of another person needing you makes you want to hide in the closet and avoid all human contact. This is normal. Whether it's the hormones that are released following childbirth, the lack of sleep, or the faltering self-confidence, getting excited about a man on top of you is the furthest thing from your mind.

That said, you can only put off your husband so long if

you hope to keep him. And while the idea of getting rid of him might sound appealing right now, it's nice to have him around for those difficult back zippers. So what can you do to overcome your newfound fear and aversion to everything pubic? The easiest way is to do the same thing you do when diving into a cold pool: Take a deep breath, close your eyes, and go for it. In the end, the result should be the same: You got wet, and it was more fun after you got used to it. But if you need a bit of a push, read on.

The "Mama Sutra"

Different things do it for different ladies. While all it takes for one woman to get in the mood is to fit back into her skinny jeans, another woman might need a full night's sleep, an elaborate island fantasy, mood lighting, and vanilla musk massage oil. We have one friend who goes absolutely weak in the knees at the sight of her husband sweeping the floor. We call this "choreplay." And even if the sight of your husband holding a broom doesn't get you going, you may want to pretend it does to get him excited about Ajaxing the sink, making the beds, and—ooh baby—emptying the diaper pail.

But if the thought of disrobing into your birthday suit instantly kills your mood, don't despair. Nobody feels great about their body after having a baby. Our breasts fall, our stomachs jiggle, and we've packed on more pounds than Renée Zellweger did when prepping for *Bridget Jones's Diary*. Some of us though are so distraught and disgusted with the aftermath of childbearing that we simply can't muster a single sexual impulse. If this sounds familiar, you need some quick strategies to get around the hump so you can start, well, humping again.

Of course, the easiest and most obvious solution is a flip of the light switch. Darkness removes inhibitions and clothing alike. But if turning off the light doesn't squelch your insecurities, there are certain sexual positions that hide stretch marks and other child-related body flaws. So the next time you need to assume a position, give one of these a spin:

A Hole in One

Wrap yourself entirely in a sheet and leave two holes, one for air and one down there.

"Don't Look Now, Butt . . ."

Sneak up behind your man, tell him to close his eyes, and give him a reach-around handy that will get him off (you).

Man's Best Friend

Doggy style requires so little effort that you could almost "play dead" while still hiding your problem area.

Laura Ingalls Goes Commando

If you happen to have a long prairie skirt or a flannel nightgown, hitch it up just enough for you to cover his wagon.

Frisky Business

We're sure you'll gladly "put your hands against the wall and spread 'em"—this gives you a chance to look as long and toned as possible, and only the wall has to witness your damaged underbelly.

Dutch Lovin'

Stand behind a Dutch door and swing open only the bottom half to "let your man in." Another plus to keep in mind is that if he can't see the top half of your body, you can use this time to catch up on your reading or give yourself a quick manicure.

Not Tonight, Dear, I Have a Deviated Cranial Lobe

New moms can have additional trouble with sex that has nothing to do with modesty. Because there are unique challenges that come with having a newborn, there are many other ~~excuses~~ reasons for putting off sex.

Pain. Even if you pass your six-week check-up with flying colors, it doesn't mean that having sex won't hurt. Between the bruising and the stitches, your genitalia feels like it's been put through a paper shredder. And if you're nursing, your vaginal walls may be thinned out and as dry as a Bond martini. If intercourse hurts, you can ease the pain by using vaginal lubricant, going slowly, and being bombed out of your mind. If months go by and you're still feeling 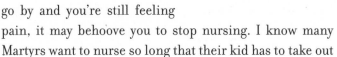 pain, it may behoove you to stop nursing. I know many Martyrs want to nurse so long that their kid has to take out his retainer before latching on, but weaning certainly takes the sting out of sex.

Exhaustion. What woman can get aroused when she's one long blink away from falling asleep standing up? And what new mom doesn't feel this way on a daily basis? Newborns are up and down all night, especially if they're breastfeeding. And even once they're old enough to sleep through the night, most Martyrs don't have the inner strength to let their poor precious babies cry it out. If you're constantly sleep deprived, you're not doing yourself or your family any good. For heaven's sake, give your kid formula at night (come and get us, La Leche League!), and let your kid learn how to put himself back to sleep when he cries. With your baby down, your husband can finally "get up," and your sex life can only get better.

Leaky breasts. If milk squirting out of your nipples during sex douses your mood, stuff your nursing bra full of Kleenex, breast pads, or hell, even tube socks. We agree that it's freaky to have dairy flow out your bosoms. It's like sneezing and having Goobers fly out. But stuff your bra and try to put it out of your mind so you can concentrate on more important things during sex. Like Matthew McConaughey's abs!

Hopefully soon, your baby will sleep more, your hormones will get back to normal, and your vaginal walls will rebuild themselves like a city post-wartime. Then, you and your lover will get down to business and things will get back to normal. Or maybe you'll still need some additional support.

Toys-Я-A-Must

Thanks to Carrie Bradshaw and Samantha Jones, the taboo regarding "sexual aides" has been lifted. Now women are free to befriend battery-operated toys that help get them through the "long winter" of celibacy and inattentive mates. Since this attitude may not have "penetrated" the walls of Martyrdom, we are here to tell you that you deserve a "Dual-Headed Jack Rabbit Vibe Max" just like the next stay-at-home mom.

If there's no amount of liquor or guilt that will coerce you through the sex shop doors, there are many online vendors or discreet catalogs that will send you whatever you desire wrapped in a nondescript brown package. Just be careful where you hide them. We had one friend who thought she'd be safe with a "lipstick" look-alike vibrator and walked in on her five-year-old daughter running the buzzing little wand over her lips exclaiming, "Mommy, this lipstick feels gooooooooood!"

If you've read and considered all of the sexual healing techniques above and still wouldn't touch Willy with a ten-foot pole, you may need additional help revving the engines of your neutral sex drive. Sometimes pregnancy does wacky things to your hormones, and you may just need some help from a professional to get your libido going (and by "professional" we are not referring to an exotic dancer from "Thunder Down Under" or "Roberto" the Italian masseur who guarantees a happy ending). Your OB/GYN can prescribe hormone supplements or creams to get your engine purring again. While you're there, pick up some birth control; another kid to a Stay-at-Home Martyr would be like throwing lighter fluid on a barbecue.

Chapter Six

Children of a Lesser Mom

There's no greater love on this planet than that of a mother for her child . . . except maybe fresh funnel cake or a deep tissue massage, but that's up for debate. We're biologically programmed to perform ridiculously selfless acts in the name of motherhood: take a bullet, hurl ourselves in front of a speeding bus, and deny ourselves any form of alcoholic beverage for forty long weeks of pregnancy (minus the first three weeks, which happened to fall over Cinco de Mayo and your best friend's bachelorette party when you were convinced the puking and sore breasts were the result of too much tequila and insufficient bra support on the dance floor). As new mothers our protective abilities become so heightened that we can sense danger, stormy weather, and poopy diapers long before they surface. In fact, if the Stay-at-Home Martyrs weren't so cemented to their glider chairs, we would say let's eighty-six the Secret Service and hand over the earpieces and black suits to the most ferocious, attentive, and protective lot in the country. Besides, everyone knows black is slimming.

While being overly capable and totally bad-ass may sound appealing, there is a flip side to all this obsessing. It's difficult to make a Martyr understand the damage she's doing to her children when she's convinced there's nothing wrong with being loving, helpful, and at their beck and call. We're sure the idea that this constant caretaking is having a detrimental effect on your kids hasn't ever crossed your mind.

Ask yourself: Do you secretly love it when your kids fall to pieces when you leave the house? Do you constantly smother them with unsolicited affection because you get so little physical contact in your own life? Are you so invested in your children's performance and success that a sub-par violin recital or a botched spelling bee sends you straight for the Prozac bottle? If so, your parenting approach may need some adjustment. The emotional and physical need is supposed to flow in one direction in a family: from the child to the parent. When a parent relies on her child for validation, success, and bragging material, the child is forced to bear the burden. This doesn't allow room for him to develop according to his own abilities and desires. And it most certainly doesn't allow room for failure, which we all know can be one of the most efficient ways to learn a lesson.

While you may think little Owen was born with the hands of an orthopedic surgeon, he may be secretly dreaming up new couture runway gown designs. Sure, all the constant doting and attention you give him may stem from love, but real love is selfless. Letting your children have their own dreams means having to find your own, and to some women this is simply too daunting. And as difficult as it may be, this means letting sweet

Owen revel in silk, satin, and vintage appliqué if that's what makes him truly happy.

You Know that You're Over-Martyring Your Kids When:
- You have an umbilical hernia from carrying your fifty-pound child around all day.

- Your kids tell YOU what to do . . . and you actually do it.

- Your kids still sleep in your bed and they have underarm hair.

- Their clothes come from Milan, yours from Marshall's.

- They get excited if they don't make the team because they know it's ice-cream time!

Who Needs Who?
The Industrial-Strength Umbilical Cord

Let us start by admitting that we totally get it. One look at your sweet little heavenly creation and even the most self-indulgent woman withers away to nothing. It makes biological sense: nature looking out for its young. If new mothers were not completely obsessed with every tiny coo or mew, babies would go uncared for.

But at some point following infancy, a healthy mother is supposed to "cut the apron strings" and let little Landon fend for himself a bit. Some mothers are able to do this with ease. The hands-off mommy with the "if-it-don't-kill-'em" attitude might feel fine leaving her two-year-old with a pizza coupon for the delivery man and the remote (which, of course, is something no one should ever do). Not the Stay-at-Home Martyr. Instead of shoving her little birdie from the nest, she would rather hand-stitch a giant double parachute and slowly cascade to the ground with her eaglet in tow. She feels that she has done the right thing by protecting her child, cushioning his fall, and staying by his side. Sadly, this little bird will not understand the principles of gravity or the importance of wing muscle development when he grows up. He will expect a homemade butt pillow at every bump in the road, and since Mom simply can't always be there to scoop him up (as much as she would love to be), he'll be left to flounder his way into adulthood.

She won't understand why he can't keep a job (he has zero ability to cope with criticism since he could do no wrong as a child). She'll be baffled by his failed relationships (he isn't capable of an empathetic emotion and can't find a woman who's willing to neglect herself to the degree that his mother was). And she'll find herself in a quandary over his unpaid parking tickets and bills (he never learned the age-old principle of cause and effect with mumsie always coming to the rescue).

You still may not believe that you can actually care too much, do too much, and love your kids too much. Scientists often study animals to learn about human behavior, so let's put a Stay-at-Home Martyr in the animal world and see how she fares. Can you imagine a mama grizzly whose cub whines incessantly until she agrees to do all the salmon catching, to collect all the berries, and to fend off all predators? Or a killer whale Martyr who spends all day boosting her calf to the surface and telling her to "blow"?

Maybe the idea is starting to sink in. Maybe you just realized that your nine-year-old has never actually brushed his own teeth. Maybe you thought it was perfectly normal that your six-year-old hyperventilates when you leave the room. Or maybe you need a little more prodding. Here's a little ditty that will resonate perhaps all too well with every Stay-at-Home Martyr:

Hush, Little Baby

Hush, little baby, don't say a word.
Mama's gotta wipe away her eight-year-old's turd.
And if you forget to brush your hair,
Mama's brought a comb so don't despair.
And if you leave your books in class,
Mama's gonna drive to school (during rush-hour traffic
for an hour) so that you'll pass.
And if your iPod Nano gets lost,
Mama'll buy you a new one despite the high cost.
And if you don't like steamed veggies and fish,
Mama'll cook you up whatever you wish.
And if you cry when it's time for bed,
Mama's gonna lie down (uncomfortably on
the floor) and rub your head.
And if you scream and stomp the ground,
She'll still think you're the sweetest little
baby in town.

We know it's hard to believe that a simple act of love can lead to such dysfunction. But we assure you that if you continue playing lifeguard/bodyguard/tutor/personal slave, you'll be denying your child one of the most important things in life: self-reliance. We're not suggesting boot camp for baby or an abrupt kick in the training pants. But little by little you need to separate. Let your child realize that the world does not self-destruct when Mommy takes a shower. Teach her that she is capable of overcoming great obstacles on her own. And start believing that you deserve a good long pee with the door closed. If you continue indulging and burdening your children with your Martyring ways, you'll be spending the rest of your time as a parent (which, consequently, is forever) dealing with the following issues.

> If you continue playing lifeguard/bodyguard/tutor/personal slave, you'll be denying your child one of the most important things in life: self-reliance.

They Won't Know How to Make Themselves Feel Better

There's nothing respectable about a man who bursts into tears when he nicks his chin shaving. Or a woman who goes ballistic when Nordstrom Rack is out of her size sandal. And nobody of substance wants to hire, marry, or befriend someone who throws himself on the floor kicking and screaming when he doesn't get the parking spot he wanted. Never learning how to cope with life's obstacles leads to the painful inability to function in the world, a lot of time and money in therapy, and resentment toward everyone's favorite target (Mom). This will continually resurface every time Junior gets fired, dumped, or denied. For these reasons and many more, kids MUST learn how to self-soothe. But how can they when the Martyr is always there to pick them up and hand them a frosted cookie?

The self-soothing process can begin as early as the birth canal. If baby has to wait thirty seconds to crown while mommy applies lipstick so she doesn't look naked, fat, AND washed out in the hospital photos, then baby will just have to learn a little patience. And while it may be true that newborns need contact, love, and security to thrive, they are also capable of relying on themselves in a variety of situations.

The most obvious way is to let them fall asleep on their own. We know it's tempting to rock your baby to sleep. To nuzzle that warm little sour milk mouth in your neck and feel like no one has ever needed or adored you more in your life. We know it's equally tempting to sleep with your baby. It's a good excuse to avoid dreaded contact with your husband, and it helps baby fall asleep happily and without migraine-inducing scream sessions. Here's why the sleepovers must stop. First, you're teaching your child that she's not capable of falling asleep on her own. By rocking her, nursing her, and lying next to her, you're basically saying, "You need me and a whole slew of soothing motions, warm elixirs, and persuasive aids in order to accomplish one of our most basic biological functions."

It all seems lovely and cozy until you begin to realize that babies go to bed earlier than adults. This translates as having to bow out of any cocktail party, dinner, juicy conversation, sexual act (gasp!), or heated game of Scattergories that might be in the works, so that lucky you can go balance on the side rail of a toddler-size bed and lie in the dark for an hour. In short, no "adult time." We know plenty of mothers (including ourselves) who have naively thought children would naturally outgrow their need for a bedtime companion. Oh, how wrong we were. Not only did our children become more needy over time, as bigger kids they were capable of getting out of bed, hunting us down, and relentlessly manipulating us like the homemade Play-Doh we make for them (even though it's only $1.49 at Target). I guarantee that your toddler will not approach you one fine evening and declare, "You know what, loving-devoted-mother-who-has-eased-me-into-sweet-slumber-over-the-past-three-years, I think I'm ready to give it a go on my own." Oh no. The nursing will become "a drink of water in my favorite cup. Not *that* favorite cup, the *other* favorite cup!" The rocking will become a twenty-minute back rub. And the lying down with them until they fall asleep will become "lying down with them until they fall asleep and staying that way in case they wake up during the night."

There are countless excuses for why we think it's okay to sleep with our kids. All as weak as the bladder of a third-time mom.

The "too lazy to formulate a decent defense" defense

"It just seems like the natural thing to do."

If we routinely based our decisions on the natural course of things, we'd all have hairy armpits, gray dreadlocks, and twenty-five kids. And let us be the first to go completely "unnatural" if it means Venus razors, highlights, Spanx, and four periods a year thanks to Seasonale. How 'bout a big hooray for the Industrial Revolution and all things manufactured?

The "chiropractically driven" defense

"It's actually been really good for my back to sleep on the wood floor in my daughter's room."

Bullshit. First off, your back only hurts because you still carry your toddler around in your New Native Baby Sling. Not to mention the forty-pound Petunia Pickle Bottom diaper bag that costs more than all the purses you've ever owned in your life combined. Second, you're lying to yourself. There is absolutely no good reason for a grown woman to be sleeping on the floor next to her child's bed. It's like the old joke; if aliens on a spaceship watched us humans picking up our dogs' poop, they'd wonder who was in charge on our planet. If they saw you sleeping on the floor covered by a Dora the Explorer beach towel next to a two-year-old snoozing on a pillow-top sleigh bed, they'd know who ruled the roost in your house. And it sure isn't you.

The "everybody's doing it" defense

"Well, in Papua New Guinea families sleep together in a one-room hut all cuddled together like a family should be."

First of all, there's no doubt that if you house-swapped with a Papua New Guinean family, they would be snoring in your California King before you could say "Hotel Collection

800-thread-count duvet cover." Second, some Papua New Guinean tribal people marry their cousins, and mothers are expected to school their sons in the art of pleasing a woman (a thought that's sure to shock even the most hardcore Stay-at-Home Martyr).

The key is to begin parenthood with the belief that your child is an individual with the ability to self-soothe. If, from the very beginning, you lay your child down when they seem tired, they quickly become familiar with the basic idea that people are supposed to lie down and fall asleep. If you don't begin the sleep training process with a solid plan, we guarantee you'll crumble and your baby will be in your bed, on your breast, or circling the block in the family sedan within a matter of minutes.

The same "self-soothing" attitude really applies in most parenting scenarios. If you rush to your child when she so much as hiccups, you're teaching her that everything is catastrophic and warrants absolute hysteria. What's the result? A child who falls apart at the sight of a hangnail. A fight on the kindergarten playground about whose favorite color is aqua? Two years of psychotherapy. We know some kids are more sensitive than others, and that some need a bit more coddling in order to feel secure in this crazy world. But wait for them to solicit your help instead of funneling your "mama's gonna make it better" mantra down their throats.

They Don't Learn How to Deal with Disappointment

No parent wants to see their child suffer, but the Stay-at-Home Martyr can't stand to see her children suffer even the slightest bit of discomfort. Every wince or whine from her offspring serves as a glaring example of her failure as a mother. Bottled water from the Swiss Alps is kept in the car in case little Juliana gets a dry mouth while on the road. Dried fruit and nut bars are kept in the purse just in case little Tate's tummy rumbles while on the go. And a first-aid kit is always kept close with an assortment of disinfectants, bee sting soothers, and favorite character boo-boo Band-Aids. But what about emotional pain? They can't let their kids suffer from that either, so if their child isn't invited to a birthday party or doesn't win first prize in the school carnival egg toss, they're consoled by a trip to the toy store. Because of this, they never learn how to pick themselves up by their imported leather boot straps and keep on keeping on.

How do we stop the madness? Here is some wisdom one woman gave us that we'll never forget. She had one of the most interesting, confident, sober, and tattoo-free teenagers we had ever met. Either she was a fantastic parent, or her son was a fantastic liar. We begged for her secret, petrified of the hormone fest that awaited us with our own children. Here's what she told us (and we swear if nothing else in this book sinks in, shoot this one directly into your frontal lobe):

> Let your kids fail. If you start letting them fail from the time they are small, they will learn the law of consequence on an equally small scale.

Let your kids fail. If you start letting them fail from the time they are small, they will learn the law of consequence on an equally small scale. For example, if your kindergartner forgets to color his apple worksheet while studying the letter "A," don't remind him repeatedly or set up the crayons, dig for the red one, bribe him to sit at the table, and then forcibly hold his hand and color the apple while he watches *The Doodlebops* in the background. I know it's close to impossible to stop yourself from saving him from failing. But simply remind him once (maybe twice if you're twitching and foaming at the mouth), and then let it go. When he remembers in the car the next morning and is scrambling to color it in, tears running down his face, he will have learned about responsibility. And the next day, he won't forget to color in that bear for "B." This small, insignificant lesson, when repeated over the course of a childhood, could save your child from having to learn the same lesson in the adult world, with adult-size consequences (i.e., a six-foot, five-inch cellmate who never made it to "C" for "Conflict Resolution" or "S" for "Shared Personal Space").

They Always Feel Like They Have to Be Good

We all know that one of the proudest moments in a mom's life is when her child goes potty for the first time. When a friend's daughter was potty training, she NEVER wanted her mom to say good job or that she was proud of her. She'd yell,

"Don't be proud, Mama, don't be proud!" Her mom realized she was putting too much pressure on her, and when the poor little thing couldn't "go," she felt like she was letting her mother down (and truth be told, she was! The woman had everything riding on that BM!). What had she done? Her poor child was going to suffer a nervous breakdown or toddler-size hemorrhoids from trying desperately to make Mommy proud.

Kids naturally want to please us. Or at least they do until they grow up and sneak off to have their nipples pierced. Instead of constantly bathing them in compliments, like "It's perfect!" "Magnificent!" "You're the best (artist, singer, musician . . .) ever!" ask questions about how *they* feel about their work instead.

"Mommy, do you like my barn?"
"Yes, Lucas, it's a great barn."
"Mommy, do you like my horse in my barn?"
"That's a lovely horse."
"Mommy, do you like my saddle on my horse in my barn?"
"What a fantastic saddle, Lucas."
"Mommy, do you like my rope on my saddle on my horse in my barn?"
"That's quite a rope."
"Is it the best you've ever seen?"
"YES! IT'S THE MOST AMAZING F-ING ROPE ON A SADDLE ON A HORSE IN A BARN I'VE EVER SEEN! NOW GO RIDE OFF INTO THE SUNSET ON IT!"

Save yourself the frustration and your child a life of neuroses and insecurity and try this script instead:

"Mommy, do you like my barn?"

"I see you spent a lot of time on that barn. It has so many different colors. What do you like about it?"

"I like that the cow and the horse get to have a sleepover."

"Do you like sleepovers?"

"Not yet, maybe when I'm seven. Or twenty-five."

"Are you done with your picture or do you still want to add more?"

"I think I want to add a chicken."

"Is the chicken going to the sleepover, too?

"No, the cow and the horse are going to eat the chicken with barbecue sauce."

"It sounds like you enjoy drawing pictures."

"Yeah, it's way funner than bedtime or taking a shower."

When children are able to develop a sense of pride in their own ability, they can rely much less on the outside world for validation. Raising them to seek approval in order to feel good about themselves only damages their potential for a secure and happy life.

They'll Grow Up Feeling Entitled

When kids are showered with every little thing they even remotely want, they develop a sense of entitlement as big as the $500 battery-powered Jeep Commando that's sitting untouched in the garage while your car is parked on the street. They don't learn to share because why the hell should they? They can have whatever they want whenever they want it. Why? Because they're *special*. We've dated guys like this, and we gotta tell ya, it ain't pretty. You can just look at them with their overconfident and arrogant ways and actually see their childhoods flash before you with doting mothers constantly telling them how wonderful they are. If you're always pumping your child full of compliments and ideas of grandeur, they'll grow to believe they're better than other people.

They can even bite a kid at the park and get away with it. Are they yelled at or punished? Nope. That'd be too cruel, too damaging to their fragile ego. Instead, the only consequence is Mommy getting down to eye level, and calmly and methodically explaining to Billy why it isn't *appropriate* to bite other people. If we have to hear the word *appropriate* one more time in our lives, we may explode into a virtual volcano of *inappropriateness*. Be serious when your kids act like little a-holes! Make them regret it if they inflict harm on others! We're not suggesting grabbing them by the pigtails and beating them over the head with your Bugaboo Frog umbrella attachment, but for the love of God, be an authority figure and teach your kids the difference between right and wrong. Figure out their currency (a certain toy, television privileges, yummy Hostess snack cakes), and when they misbehave, take them away. Teach them that, just like in real life, there are consequences for their actions.

Kids of this generation are constantly overindulged and believe that they should never lose, never have to suffer, and never have to cope with disappointment. Can you imagine a society where everyone believes they're *special?*

Who's going to pick up the trash when everyone thinks they deserve their own reality show on E!? Who's going to deliver the mail and clean the roads and grow the food if the general population is holding out for the corner office everyone told them they deserve? We live in an age where nobody gets left behind and self-esteem rules. We're not suggesting that these things are bad; clearly these are noble and worthy causes. We are simply pointing out that there's a flip side to always getting a trophy whether you win or lose. This isn't the way the real world works, and kids are then left unable to cope with criticism, mediocrity, and failure.

They Won't Learn How to Be Independent

Beyond not having the ability to reach around and give themselves an emotional pat on the back, kids raised in the realm of the Martyr also won't have the ability to "take care of business" independently. Remember that pathetic scene in *Sixteen Candles* where a set of fed-up parents forcibly shove their geeky son into the school dance, then hold the doors shut while he pounds and wails, "But I want to stay home! I want to be with you guys!" As hilarious as that was on-screen, we guarantee you won't be thrilled when it's your own inept kid getting pummeled by Jake Ryan and paying a dollar in the boy's bathroom to get a glimpse of sexy girl undies (Lord knows he's only seen granny panties in the hamper at home).

You may be wondering, "How does this happen? One minute I'm zipping up my little boy's sweater and the next minute I'm picking up his man underwear despite an arthritic back and mild dementia." This ineptitude is brought on as a result of all the "wonderful things" you're doing ~~to~~ for your children.

Let's talk about separation. We know you have a dreadful fear of leaving your children in the hands of others. There is no one as qualified as you to keep them safe . . . not even their own fathers. But if they haven't been apart from you in the first five years of life, you can't expect them to saunter into kindergarten and plop down for circle time, eager to shine as the "Star of the Week" and tackle whatever lowercase letter is tossed their way. Instead, that little creature of yours will be suctioned to your body like a Tiny Love Froggle bath toy. There are many ways to offer your child freedom and independence. Here are some important ways to begin the separation process.

You're Mad for Fashion

Beyond separating physically, your child needs to flex his mental autonomy from time to time. As we all know, young children like to choose things: which color bowl, which seat in the booth, which bedtime book, and most importantly, which clothes to wear. Yes, the clothes. Nothing says independence more than choosing one's own outfit. But, as anyone with kids knows, preschoolers exist in a fashion world all of their own. As difficult as it may be, you must come to terms with the fact that what you find pleasing to the senses is not necessarily what is *en vogue* on the playground. While polka-dot velvet pants and a princess gown may offend your sensibilities, it's met with a slew of oohs and ahhs at the finger painting easel.

We know it's challenging to let your three-year-old accompany you to the market in a too-tight Power Rangers costume (that he's worn for four days straight). You're probably of the philosophy that a well-dressed child reflects well on Mom (despite the fact that you have no problem leaving the house in what you wore to bed). If Mom gathers all her self-worth through her offspring, a mismatched outfit is like a punch in the face. A stained Pocahontas sweatshirt? A left hook to the chin. Torn Batman pajamas and rain boots? One final jab to the gut and she's down for the count.

Our friend Hillary fought like you would not believe to get her daughter to wear beautiful (costly) British apparel she had imported while pregnant. She would literally hold her daughter down and shove her limbs into the most adorable corduroy paisley pants, starched white butterfly collar blouse, and patent Mary Janes. This child scratched and tore at the outfit like it was made of thorns (and the coordinating paisley headband was immediately ripped from her head and tossed like a one-way boomerang). This went on for weeks until Hillary simply couldn't cope with another morning of wailing, coercing, and tantruming (from herself or her daughter). She stared at the moaning, writhing little demon on her bedroom floor and declared defeat. "Fine, wear whatever you want."

The wailing instantly ceased.

Her daughter looked over at her, baffled. "Really?"

Hillary conceded. For the next two weeks her daughter wore one outfit only: a beaded lavender tank top, leopard leggings, and blue cowgirl boots. As nauseating as it was, our friend swallowed all pride and (wisely) decided to see where things headed. On the thirteenth day, her daughter emerged in a floral cardigan and jeans. She paused in front of her mom and with a concerned look on her little face asked, "Do I look *fashion* to you?"

Hillary had wised up. "Do you *want* to look fashion?" Her daughter nodded.

Hillary smiled. "Absolutely *fashion*. But what about your favorite pants and boots?"

Her daughter considered the question. "Sofie saw a leopard at the zoo that had a weird yucky bump on its face. Leopards are ugly. Flowers are *fashion*." She struck a pose, spun on her red glittery "Dorothy" heels and was out the door. It had all been about power and autonomy and was probably only the first of many situations that would require Hillary to step back and let her daughter find a place in the world as a powerful individual.

Most moms we know agree that one rule worth enforcing is that clothing must be "seasonally appropriate." You simply can't leave the house mid-January in a coconut-shell bikini top and grass skirt. One mom's four-year-old solved that dilemma by putting thermal long-johns UNDER her hula ensemble. Who can argue with such highly developed problem-solving skills?

The Rescuers
. . . .

Another important part of raising independent kids is to stop coming to the rescue. Obviously we're not referring to turning a cheek when your child is practicing cartwheels at the edge of the Grand Canyon. We're simply referring to letting your child learn and problem solve on his own whenever possible.

As infants, we sit our babies in those Bumbo-Mumbo-Jumbo chairs when they cry instead of letting them build the muscles to roll, then move, and then sit. As toddlers, we help them walk by holding their hands over their head, which leads to kids who reach up while falling instead of using their hands to balance themselves and break their many falls. In short, don't be a prosthetic limb. If they aren't walking yet, let them crawl until they get up and experiment with a few wobbly steps on their own. If they get stuck, talk them through how to get unstuck on their own.

The "rescue me" scenario presents itself over and over when you have young kids. We met one mom whose seventeen-month-old's idea of playing catch was to throw the ball, then look at her, point at it, and repeat a whiny "eh, eh, eh, eh, eh" until she retrieved it for him. He would then throw it and do it all again. She thought it was a cute little game until she noticed he was devolving into a lazy Neanderthal baby. If he was thirsty, he would point at his cup (on the tray four inches in front of him), "eh, eh, eh, eh, eh, eh." If he wanted her to read him a book, he would sit down against the bookshelf, wrinkle his nose, and point at the books, "eh, eh, eh, eh, eh." She quickly put a kibosh on the caveman. Her general rule about whining (which we find quite brilliant) is that she only tolerates it if it's her fault. If kids are suffering low blood sugar because parents haven't fed them, or if they're overtired because parents failed to put them to bed on time, then they have full whining rights. Other than that, there is a strict policy against all screechy, grating, and melodramatic manners of communicating. With her son she simply told him, "The book/ball/cup is right in front of you. If you want it, get it." Then she redirected her attention to something else and lo and behold, he would happily grab it and move on.

This could have easily turned into her catering to the every grunt of her increasingly inept little boy. And the result may have been a life of frustrated teachers and a miserable wife who would scream at him before speeding off with the kids, the dog, and the china, "Eh yourself, you bastard!"

So as easy as it is for you to quickly zip up your five-year-old's sweater, button her pants, or tie her shoes, encourage her to try. Let her get frustrated. And then encourage her to try again.

Lost in Translation

We're all guilty of this one. We talk for our kids. We want them to communicate with the outside world like adults, so we respond for them when people ask, "How are you?" "What would you like to drink?" "What's your name?" etc. It starts when they're babies and can't yet strike up a conversation on their own. We are their natural interpreters. But then the situation snowballs and we become parent ventriloquists. And when the time comes for our kids to talk for themselves, they can't. We end up with children who are perma-glued to the backs of our legs while we jabber on about what they want to drink, what their names are, and how they feel. Not only does this undermine their developing language skills and confidence, it's really quite disrespectful. Why do we think we always know how our children feel? And how will they ever have the emotional intelligence to know the difference between sad/angry/jealous/frustrated if we don't help them identify these feelings?

Of course there's always that awkward moment when a well-meaning elderly woman at the supermarket approaches your three-year-old and says, "Well, hello there. Aren't you the cutest thing? Are you a good helper to your mommy?" And your kid stares silently, eyes fixed on the giant liver spot spreading across the woman's face. You're positive that if you don't respond immediately your child's response will be, "What's that gross thing on your head?" Clearly this would be an appropriate time to interject, "She's a wonderful helper! Have a lovely day." And then quickly grab your kid and run to safety in the diaper aisle. Oh, wait, the diaper aisle may not be clear of old ladies either.

So how do we teach our kids to self-soothe, deal with disappointment, feel less pressure, stop feeling entitled, and become independent without being negligent or overly authoritative? How do we (as Stay-at-Home Martyrs) care a little bit less about them and a little bit more about ourselves without being selfish? We show them that it's perfectly acceptable to take care of ourselves. That it's equally acceptable to be flawed. We treat them with respect but don't cherish every word that comes out of their mouths. Generally speaking, we lower the bar a notch and just let them be.

Lowering the Bar to Raise Happier Kids

There's a saying we heard that's stuck with us: "Kids are like pancakes. You should be able to throw the first one away." As anyone knows who's ever made pancakes from scratch (and what true Stay-at-Home Martyr hasn't?), the first one never comes out quite right. The pan isn't hot enough so they tend to be gooey on the inside and not nicely browned. Parents tend to be the most nervous and unsure with their firstborn, so they make the most mistakes. They don't mean to. It's just that their pan isn't hot enough from lack of experience. This would imply that one way to stop the madness of Martyrdom is to keep having babies. Your first kid slept in a Bambino crib with French bumpers and a cashmere blanket. Your second kid gets it all "hand-me-down" with the handcrafted rails now covered in teething gnaw marks and the cashmere now torn from getting caught under the stroller wheel one too many times. By the third kid, you simply pull out a sock drawer, line it with a beach towel, and call it a bed.

Really, overpopulation and depletion of Earth's natural resources aside, what better way to solve the problem of Martyrdom than having *more* children? Okay, some of you may argue that baby making isn't the most conscientious remedy. So here are a few other ways to lower your standards and raise happier kids.

> Let your kids have space to ding their doors. Teach them that imperfection can be beautiful and valuable. Nobody's good at everything. How boring would the world be if everything was shiny, perfect, and exactly the same?

Just like getting your first "door ding" on a new car, once you accept that your child isn't perfect, you can just sit back and enjoy the ride. Let your kids have space to ding their doors. And not only that, but teach them that imperfection can be beautiful and valuable. Nobody's good at everything. And how boring would the world be if everything was shiny, perfect, and exactly the same?

Kids can sniff out authenticity like a bloodhound in a Jamaican airport baggage terminal. They know when we're really listening and when we are just nodding while focusing on the new Pottery Barn catalog. A friend's nine-year-old was whining and begging her mother to let her go on an overnight trip to Disneyland with a family she had barely met. The answer was no. She begged on, hoping she could wear mom down with guilt-inducing tactics. Clearly the mother's approach was not having the desired effect of her daughter accepting the decision and then commending her mom on having such good parental instincts. She decided to give her daughter a choice. Curious to see which she would prefer, she offered her two styles of "mothering." The first was careful, sensitive, and articulate.

"Honey, I know you really love fast rides, sugar highs, and wanna-be actresses painted up like mermaids and ball-going belles, but there is simply no way that I am going to feel comfortable letting you go that far away for two days with a family I've spoken to once at a school pizza night. I know you're disappointed, but believe me when I tell you that it's for the best."

The second approach was a bit more to the point: "Over my dead body."

The daughter decided she liked the second choice better because it "wasn't all fake." (But she still wanted to know if maybe mom could call and talk to the parents and then if they weren't totally weird could she still go?) The point is kids like honesty. It doesn't always make them like you, but deep down they appreciate the fact that they can rely on you to be straightforward and authentic. In addition to keeping it real, try to focus on the effort rather than results. A valiant effort is far nobler than an easy "A." Maybe not as appreciated by the University Admissions System, but valiant nonetheless. Kids know when you're heavily invested in their success. So underneath that triple-decker ice cream sundae and Cheshire grin you have plastered to your face, little Jonah knows you actually *do* care that he didn't win class president. And despite your telling him repeatedly that he was a *way* better candidate than Emily B. and that being president means having to miss recess once a week, so good thing he didn't win, he's disappointed. And he knows you're disappointed too. Instead of trying to "turn that frown upside down," let him wallow, let him say how he feels, and then tell him a story about how you failed miserably at something when you were his age. Most kids will appreciate bedtime stories that revolve around "Embarrassing Things that Happened to Mom and Dad When They Were Growing Up" including such classics as: wetting the bed at a sleepover, expelling gas during the holiday program, spelling the word "spelling" wrong in the spelling bee, etc.

Another major way of relieving pressure in the household is to make free time. Cancel all appointments. Let the minds wander. Let the imaginations grow. Many mommies out there have a morbid fascination with "enrichment activities." They schedule class upon class, trying to nurture every nugget of raw talent or interest into full-fledged Olympic training. The result: a kid who has no down time to just be, and a Martyr who's crazed from trying to balance after-school lessons and activities with homework, family time, bath time, and meal time.

You Know You're Obsessed with Extracurricular Activities When . . .

- Your four-year-old shows you her "new move" that resembles a karate chop with jazz hands, and the next day she's enrolled in Tuesday/Thursday martial arts and Monday/Wednesday hip-hop.

- While listening to Raffi, your son cuts the rug a la Elaine from *Seinfeld*, so it's off to Twyla Tharp for Toddlers class for the next twelve-week session.

- Your seven-year-old has a great time at an ice-skating party. Convinced there's a young Michelle Kwan in there just waiting to come out, you set your alarm for 4:00 a.m. and head to the rink to start her training.

- You enroll your one-year-old in Baby's First Chinese Class because you can't stand the fact that your neighbor's kid speaks fluent Mandarin, despite the fact that he's from China and you're not.

We all love our kids. We sign them up for overpriced, time-consuming activities because we want them to have every opportunity in life. We hope they win class president because we want them to know they are capable of accomplishing great things. We hold them too much and cuddle them tighter than we should because we want them to believe that the world is a safe and nurturing place. But the reality is that the world is only sometimes a safe and nurturing place. And while they *are* capable of accomplishing great things, they're also capable of making irreversible bad decisions. Occasionally nudging them away from us and letting them cope with the aftermath of their decisions is an incredibly loving (and difficult) thing to do. It will give them valuable tools they need as adults.

They are individuals with their own set of passions, flaws, and plans. And while we cringe every time a wedding ceremony pulls out a Kahlil Gibran and "speaks to us of marriage," we have to acknowledge how right he was about children. "Our children come through us, but not from us."

We know it's going to be difficult to let go. Freeing yourself from addiction is never easy; just ask half your high-school buddies. It would be lovely if there was an "I'm-too-attached patch" or "Martyr-Mum-Gum" that could wean you off your kids. Maybe what you need is a project. Something to distract you from the fact that little Celeste is wearing two different-colored socks and little Milo is learning how to get down from the kitchen counter all by himself. Maybe it's time to tackle the household.

Chapter Seven

Home Is Where the Martyr Is

Upon entering the home of a Stay-at-Home Martyr, one is immediately struck by the eclectic pairings of this emerging design style. Who knew that among interiors such as "Traditional," "Mid-Century Modern," "Colonial Revival," and "French Provincial" was "Kid Crap Everywhere"? It's shabby without the chic. If one were to try to describe the essence of this predominantly suburban trend, one might say it looked as if Toys Я Us vomited in every room of the house.

You'll notice that, despite the growing numbers of homes done in this uniquely nauseating style, there's an absence of interior design publications celebrating the look. When was the last time you came across one of the following at the newsstand?

- *House and KinderGarten*: a magazine devoted to organizing the mountains of toys and child-related crap you have lying around the house.

- *Parkitectural Digest*: a publication for the mom who wants to maximize her outdoor play area. This month features "Feng Shui Play: How to classically arrange your home swing, slide, and sandbox to enrich health, wealth, and your child's joy."

· *Elle-M-N-O-P Decor*: Learn to incorporate school curriculum in your home furnishings. From framed wall art that encourages phonetic awareness to toilet paper rolls printed with the ABCs, we've got it all!

· *Cottage (Cheese) Living*: No, it's not about the cellulite on the back of your thighs. This one's about all the crumbs, food stains, and pieces of dried-out string cheese living in the cracks of your cushions. Whether it be your car, your couch, or your purse, you've got a science experiment around every corner!

· *Metropolitan Homeschooled*: Who needs the Ivy League when they've got you?! Keep your "one-room schoolhouse" fully stocked with the latest and greatest in homeschooling. Need more space? This month's edition will show you how to "turn your master bedroom into the U of M.O.M you've always dreamed of."

The reason such titles don't exist is that they shouldn't. Homes are not amusement parks. Amusement parks are amusement parks. Homes are sanctuaries that adults own and children get to live in until they are old enough to go away. If you work yourself to the bone trying to make sure that every square inch of your home caters to your child's need for constant entertainment, not only will she never develop an imagination, she will also never leave. And while this may be your secret fantasy, she needs to forge her own path (go to Mexico and drink cheap beer until she pukes), experiment with possibilities (become a vegan and develop deep disdain toward all things leather), and discover what makes her happy (a boyfriend with a tongue piercing who hasn't spoken to his family in seven years). Your home hasn't always been Funland. There was a time when it was yours. A time when you were reckless enough to have a white sofa and breakable dinnerware. Remember the clank of metal on porcelain? Those were the days . . . (Cue wavy "go back in time" effect.)

> Homes are not amusement parks. Homes are sanctuaries that adults own and children get to live in until they are old enough to go away.

Back in the De-cor

There was a time when you would leave your house and come back to find everything exactly as you left it. When a glass of red wine on the coffee table wouldn't trigger your internal danger alarm. When the sharp corners of the coffee table wouldn't send you on red alert. But those days are long gone. No longer do logs crack and burn in the hearth. No longer do plants bloom and thrive in handmade ceramic pots (unless you count those Chia-pet creatures with crazy sprout hair your child forgets to water). And no more do cool breezes blow lazily through screenless windows (one stanza of Eric Clapton's "Tears in Heaven" and all access to fresh air was abandoned in favor of giant Plexiglas and prison-bar window coverings). How did this happen? One day you could open the toilet seat with a pinky finger, and now lifting the lid requires the logic power of solving the Rubik's Cube blindfolded.

As much as the Stay-at-Home Martyr obsesses over her children, she's lost control over her household. We're not referring to cleanliness. Lord knows she can spot a germ across a dark room that most people could only detect with a high-powered lab microscope.* And we're not referring to disorganization either. The sales guy does a happy dance every time she walks into The Container Store knowing his monthly commission just tripled. No, we're referring to the general "kid-centric" style of the Stay-at-Home Martyr-run household. It's like stepping into a nightmare where big people no longer rule and everyone's left with their feet hanging off the ends of tiny beds and their butts struggling to stay on pint-size potty seats. Maybe a guided tour of "Casa Martyr" will better illustrate the magnitude of kid-centric living that has emerged.

You Know You've Decorated in "Kid Crap Everywhere" When . . .

- Your living room coffee table is a train table boasting a roundhouse, suspension bridge, and a variety of colorful trains with British accents.

- The good china you bust out at formal occasions is decorated with Sesame Street characters and each plate is a different primary color.

---

*Refer to the "Germs Are Good (and Other Reasons to Stop Cleaning Your House)" section in this chapter.

- Every sheet in the house (including yours) is backed with squeaky waterproof vinyl. Which means that every time someone rolls over in the night, it wakes everybody up.

- Your dining room chandelier is now a Baby Einstein Discover & Play Musical Mobile. It may be too dark to see what you're eating at dinner, but at least baby's happy.

- Your relaxing whirlpool tub has been transformed into a freakin' fun zone complete with soap finger paints, singing dolphins, and a giant plastic duckie covering your $700 vintage tub spout from Waterworks.

Preschool of Interior Design

Inside the home, all breakables have been sent to the island of misfits, and molded plastic furnishings have taken their place. Coffee tables are now distant memories, along with side tables, console tables, or any other solid surface on which a person could set a beverage. Of course, that really isn't an issue considering that no open containers are allowed within a ten-foot radius of little Amelie. Unless of course it's in a spill-proof cup, "which is a great idea because if we all drink out of them, she'll be even more encouraged to stop using the bottle. I mean, when she's ready of course."

Since so many of the furnishings have been stored in the garage or sold on eBay to fund bigger and better kid crap, you may be wondering what furniture could possibly be left. The couch! Oh wait, can't sit there because little Wilder has made a Mars Rovercraft out of it, and you promised you would "save it" until he was done. Well, it's been a month now, and he's still not done. But your husband is. He wants nothing more than to sit down and read a book for ten minutes before going to bed. He finally snaps and hurls all the Rover pillows, blankets, and space shuttle sheets onto the family room floor. Sadly though, after doing so, he noticed a nasty array of mysterious child-related stains, smudges, scents, and particles that sent him right past wailing Wilder and toward the only available seating in the house . . . *le toilette* (and since no one can actually open the damn thing anymore, it serves as a lovely reading chair).

The furniture isn't the only part of the room that's been taken over by your kid. So has the artwork. Granted, we are all our children's biggest fans. Every step they take is like man's first lunar stride. Every brushstroke at the preschool easel conjures images of Michelangelo's Sistine Chapel. But as proud as you are of your child's artistic ability, there's simply no need to spend mounds of money framing every Jackson Pollock-like piece of splatter art that comes home from preschool. Yes, it's cute. Yes, it should be preserved and enjoyed for years to come. But that's what refrigerators and baby books are for. No dinner party guest wants to be stared down by a 20 x 30 framed and matted "Gobble the Thanksgiving Handprint Turkey."

Whatever wall space your kid's artwork hasn't consumed, their photographs have. Your home is like an Ansel Adams exhibition, only substitute your kid's face where a Monterey pine used to be. A portrait here or there is fine. A few staggered ones on a wall shelf or console table. A nightstand perhaps. Even the hallway can make a lovely family photo gallery. But that's where the exhibit should end. You might be thinking, "Who cares if I have a custom shopping bag with my child's face blown up to cover the entire bag?" Or "What's the big deal if my coffee mug, T-shirt, wall calendar, stationery, playing cards, cell phone screen, and bracelet charms all celebrate my darling offspring?" There is nothing inherently wrong with any of these items individually. In fact, a shiny bracelet charm reminding you of the day little Rosie got her first tooth will always bring a smile to your face. It's the psychology of excessive child fixation that's worrisome. It's frightening to think that you're so dedicated to your children that they now dominate your visual field at all times. What's next? A giant mural of little Ashlynn on the dining room wall? An elaborate tattoo of little Preston on your bicep?

It begs the question: Have you lost the ability to find joy in other worldly pleasures? Does the first sign of spring only remind you of little Zoe's allergies? Does the first photo taken atop Mt. Everest only send you on a rant about inadequate safety measures? Does delicate jazz composition only remind you to call little Walker's clarinet teacher to reschedule? If so, you've lost sight of the emotional significance of life's natural beauty. You've forgotten that little joys hide around every corner, not just in the three-foot radius that surrounds your child. It's time to look around and see what's out there. You don't have to be an art connoisseur to bring sophistication into your home.

You just have to do it. In terms of wall decor, it can be as simple as going online or into a frame store and buying a nice copy of Van Gogh's *Starry Night* or Gustav Klimt's *The Kiss*. Mount it in an elegant frame and let your imagination wander. Talk to your child about the artist. Show them that it's okay to appreciate other people's talents and not just to be appreciated. Maybe it'll even inspire you to take a watercolor class. Or at the very least, it'll remind you that having a sense of wonder about the world is not reserved for those under age ten.

Less Is More than Enough

We would all agree that making your home relatively child-friendly and safe is a good idea. Put that decorative bowl filled with chokeable marbles up on the high shelf. Lock up that gun cabinet and throw away the bullets. And the outdoor fire pit should probably remain unlit for a few years. These are reasonable ways to ensure your child's safety. But the Stay-at-Home Martyr has taken this to such an extreme that every drawer, cupboard, stairway, and point of entry has become virtually inaccessible as a result of babyproof mania. Getting into the house shouldn't require *Mission Impossible*-esque feats of strength, cunning, and

> Let's babyproof only what's necessary and believe in our children's ability to decipher danger from safety, and good behavior from "you're in deep doo-doo now, mister" behavior.

flexibility. And God forbid if a guest had a headache under your roof. By the time you'd manage to get the cabinet lock open, the drawer safety latch unhooked, the medicine lock box combo set cracked (having to try every kid's birth date before getting the right one), and the childproof cap off the bottle of aspirin, you'd both have a full-blown migraine. Obviously, with young children on the prowl we don't want explosives, glass shards, and poison lying around the house on low shelves. But there is something to be said for letting kids learn from their mistakes. The world is not one large padded room (except for a small sub-population who may have attended one too many gynecological exams with their mothers). So let's teach our kids the principles of gravity, inertia, and cause and effect. Let's babyproof only what's necessary and believe in our children's ability to decipher danger from safety, and good behavior from "you're in deep doo-doo now, mister" behavior.

While most of the home can be emptied of some of the baby gates, bumper pads, and foam floor puzzles, we've found that it's a great idea to have at least one room in the house that is entirely childproof. This way if you lock yourself out of the house while retrieving little Wade's "pookie-blankey" in the backseat of the car, you can rest assured that he won't be hurling himself out a window or playing "Benihana Man" with Mommy's steak knives. This is the one room where you're free to unlock your inner preschool teacher. Let loose the toy caddies, rounded edges, super play yard XT baby corral, and a boatload of microfiber, stain-resistant fabrics. It should be noted that, if possible, this room should be hidden from the entryway and needs a door that can be closed securely and completely forgotten when children are not present.

That said, the rest of your house should not look like an f-ing Chuck E. Cheese! For one thing, having a house scattered with toys isn't safe and turns a home into a landmine. One could get impaled by stepping on a Polly Pocket or sitting on a Captain Hook figurine. Not only do toys pose a physical threat, but certain ones pose a mental threat as well. We'd like to declare a moratorium on any and all toys that talk, laugh, honk, beep, flash, or sing. Since when does a shape sorter have to congratulate the child in both English and Spanish for shoving the circle in the circle hole? And then break into song over and over: "Hooray, hooray, hooray, today's your special day, you put the shape in just the right way, HEY!" And if the cheesiness alone doesn't raise a generation of singing and clapping lame-os, then they'll all fall over at an early age from lead-based painted toys made in China.

While on the subject of toys, let's talk about what constitutes a worthwhile purchase. You already know our position on toys that make noise. The other thing to consider when browsing the toy aisle is whether it's a toy that leaves room for the child to actually play with it. The majority of toys on the market now are "closed-ended," meaning they have one purpose. Push the button and watch Spiderman do the web-dance. Dump all the puzzle pieces on the floor and then put it back together (except for that one piece that's been missing since five minutes after you bought it). It's okay to have these single-task toys, but the majority of what your playroom has to offer should be "open-ended." These are toys that can be used in many ways, for many years. Some examples include arts and crafts supplies, scarves, blocks, easels, and dramatic play items. This is important for two reasons. One, the toy will not be used once and then tossed in the back of the closet where it will suddenly "come to life" and announce at 2:00 a.m. at high volume, "Score, a direct hit! Way to go, little slugger!" The other reason to stick with the open-ended items is that they encourage creative and critical thinking. Hell, requiring any form of thought or activity is a plus in this age of fat-kid entertainment. We can't tell you how many hours kids spend at their play kitchens, which transform into restaurants, then the doctor's office, then a science experiment center. We're sure in the teenage years it'll serve as a lovely meth lab, but hey, at least we'll have gotten well beyond our $100 worth of use out of it!

Like most of the messages in this book, whether it be babyproofing or toys, less is more. Kids can sit around a room so full of toys that it looks like they live in the Target toy section, and complain that they're bored. One mom's favorite retort, "If you're bored, you're boring." To this kids usually sigh dramatically and then turn it up a notch, "What should I *dooooooooo?*" One day, after one such interaction, she got so frustrated with their whining, she shoved all the toys in large Hefty bags and told them she was giving them to deserving children. They cried as she, like Santa on Opposites Day, dragged a black sack of toys *out* of the house. She was determined to teach them a lesson.

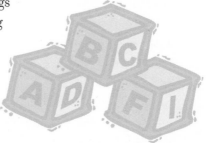

Ha! Now they'll suffer. Now they'll understand just how lucky they are to have so many things to play with! But it seems she was the one who learned a lesson because after two minutes of sulking in an empty room, they regrouped and began a Sea World performance extravaganza that required a dolphin and whale puppet made from the socks they were wearing and ample space to perform death-defying somersaults and couch dives. Who knew that an empty room could provide so much more inspiration than a room drowning in toys?

So babyproof selectively, rid your house of landmines, and mute any toy that is capable of making a sound. And remember, just as good play comes from rooms free of overstimulation, good "adult time" comes from rooms free of kids altogether.

The White Zone Is for Immediate Loading and Unloading of Kid Crap Only

Every home deserves a red zone. We're not suggesting that you shriek every time your child leaves a footprint on your living room rug. Houses are for living in. But we are recommending that at the end of the day, you put away everything that smells of child and pretend you are a young, powerful, childless executive or model or artist who has yet another evening to entertain herself. It doesn't have to be the whole house. Pick an area, and when the kids have had all their drinks, stories, back rubs, trips to the bathroom (from all the drinking), and are finally snoring away in La La Land, shove everything child-related in a cabinet and do something adult.

For one mom we know, it's the "beige zone." When she's unwinding at the end of a tiring day, she doesn't want to see a single primary color. She wants at least thirty minutes where all she sees is neutral. Give her "taupe" or "sand," even a "charcoal" or "slate," and she's a new woman. For another mom, it's the master bedroom. Every night before she goes to bed, she sweeps down her room of all child paraphernalia. She can't fall asleep if she knows there's a box of wipes on the floor by her nightstand. So much as a plastic toddler hair clip under her bed will keep her mind reeling all night. While she may be in need of some OCD treatment, she has a point.

Assuming you're not still doing the whole "family bed" thing since you're so far along in this book, keep the master bedroom exclusively adult. Who can rally a sexual thought when surrounded by Webkinz, a Gymini Activity Center, and a Nature's Best Papasan Infant Swing? How many times has your husband rolled over in bed to tell you he loves you (translation: "Wanna do it?") only to find himself lying on top of a hard plastic Dora doll instead of you? Apparently Dora doesn't enjoy your husband's meager attempts at exploration any more than you do, as she manages a "Come on, vamanos, get off me, you fat-ass" while being squished by 200 pounds of man-flesh.

Once the toys are out of there, turn your neglected master suite into an inviting romantic retreat. Invest in a few scented candles, new curtain panels, perhaps a fresh duvet cover and some decorative pillows, and most importantly: GOOD LIGHTING. Not only is it easy on tired eyes, it will make you look WAY better naked. The key is to make it enticing and warm and somewhere you look forward to retiring after a long day.

Home may be where the heart is, but after a trying day of child supervision, peace at home is found in a kid-free zone. A place where you can finish a thought and relax your mind, even for just a few minutes. And if you can't find a nook inside to call your own, let's go outside and see if we can find one there.

Nature vs. Nurturing Our Young

Once upon a time there was a lovely rose and herb garden, birds that chirped, tulips that bloomed, and morning glory vines that stretched out across the great expanse of your backyard. It was a time when people wandered into the garden for a moment of peace. Of reflection. On summer nights you ate leisurely outside and the only thing that interrupted your idyllic communion with Mother N. was the occasional bug zap in the background.

Somehow between that moment of summer lovin' and now, kid paraphernalia popped up all over your yard like those mysterious mushrooms that seem to appear overnight. What was once your botanical haven is now a Little

Tikes plastic graveyard. Most plant life has been ripped from the ground to eliminate all possible toxins and chokeable items such as inedible berries, flowers, rocks, pebbles, seed pods, etc. All plants with thorns have been extricated, as well as any flowering bush that attracts bees. You cut back all vines, hedges, and shrubbery to allow room for a monstrous jungle gym, and what's left of your lawn has been killed by your kiddie pool that leaves a circle of death in its path. If you're lucky enough to have an actual pool, you must put up a giant pool perimeter fence system (ugly and costly), as well as some kind of netting or pool cover (also ugly and costly) that's such a pain in the ass to remove, it deters everyone from even using the pool. And don't forget the pool alarm that blares through the neighborhood, often in the middle of the night, if anything heavier than a handful of leaves ever falls in the water.

What was once a haven for all forms of wildlife, from squirrels to hummingbirds to butterflies, now stands lifeless like one of those movies from the future where only a handful of people survive. No plant life means no watering, so the ground critters caravanned elsewhere. And the only bird calls you hear come from the Big Bird Water-Wham-O-Sprinkler that sings while soaking both you and your outdoor patio furniture. On a rare occasion, you may encounter a neighbor's cat that comes to your yard to use your giant sandbox, or as he calls it, outdoor plumbing.

After all this, what's left of your outdoor sanctuary? Absolutely nothing. Like everything else, you gave it all away in the name of your kids. Will your children get to watch things bloom in the spring? No. Will they learn to treat plant life delicately and with care? No. Will they learn how things grow seasonally? No. Instead, they'll continue on with their skewed belief that everyone and everything is designed for them. And when their kindergarten teacher asks them where fruits and vegetables come from, they'll say, "Gelson's Market" (or whatever overpriced gourmet grocery that has opened in your neck of the woods).

On the Road

The other place the Stay-at-Home Martyr spends a good portion of her time is in the car. We're not talking about cruising with the top down, music thumping as your hair blows wildly on the open road. We're talking about a minivan loaded with screaming, whining kids, *Dan Zane's House Party* booming on the stereo, and a backseat full of travel games, DVDs, Gameboy chargers, outlets, art materials, and on-the-go snack baskets. The trunk is loaded with waterproof play blankets, scooters, first-aid kits, diapers, SPF 50 sun tents, and strollers. And that's not even addressing the fact

The good news is that if you were ever trapped in the car during a snowstorm or heat wave, you could survive for months using the goods you tote around on a daily basis.

that there are fermented grapes, aged cheese, Cheerios, and myriad unidentifiable food scraps in every crack, door handle, and carpet gap. The good news is that if you were ever trapped in the car during a snowstorm or heat wave, you could survive for months using the goods you tote around on a daily basis. Call it "emergency preparedness" if you like, but to most of the world it looks like a rotting, three-ring circus on wheels.

There may be no way around the fact that you need seating for seven in your vehicle. But you can make some changes to dramatically improve the many hours you spend driving to and from every child-related activity under the sun.

- Clean out the stinking car. Leave one stroller, a small basket of toys, a first-aid kit if you must, some water, and a couple Cliff bars. When your kids bring toys on the road, make them bring them inside when you get home. Otherwise the cycle just begins again.

- Get a couple of CDs that remind you of being young and skinny and free and crank 'em up in the carpool line. There's no better way to jump-start a desire to get in shape than remembering lovers of years past.

- Go online and buy a few books on CD and maybe even a Pimsleur Foreign Language CD set. With all the time you spend at the wheel, you could be fluent in four languages by the time your kids hit middle school.

- Claim the front end of the car as yours. Remember, it is actually yours! Keep your favorite lip gloss, hand cream, nail file, and magazine in the driver-side door. Then, when you're stuck waiting at Junior Gym, you can improve the ragged, dirty nail situation, get some home decor ideas, and moisturize the lips. Also, keep a bottle of water in your drink holder. Nothing spells headache like a day of dry, hot carpooling without hydration.

It's little acts like these that make a woman feel like an adult with her own set of needs. It also demonstrates to the kids that mommies are people with musical tastes, dry lips, and a flair for second language acquisition, too. (Who knew?!)

Other Living Creatures

While you may believe that your family consists of just you and your kids (oh, and that guy who makes those gross noises next to you when he sleeps), you probably host a whole subculture of living creatures who are suffering the wrath of Martyrdom as well. Sadly, they have no good defense. There are no houseplant help lines or hungry pet advocacy groups. They have to simply sit back and wait for every scrap of love and attention you throw their way. Well, we are here to speak out as the first "other living creature" advocate. And after years of neglect, we're sorry to say, they're totally pissed.

The Ficus in the Corner

Take a look at your ficus. Not long ago, you'd shine her leaves, bathe her in sunlight, and feed and water her regularly. But now she's covered in dust and cobwebs, her leaves are brittle due to dehydration, and, since the high chair took over her coveted spot in the bright corner, she's had less sunlight than a woman recovering from a laser peel. If she could speak, she'd tell you that you should be ashamed of yourself, shoving another juice box down your kid's throat while she hasn't had a drink since the cat peed in her planter.

The Fish

As if the goldfish don't have it hard enough trying to stay alive longer than their usual forty-eight-hour life span, they've now been quarantined to a high shelf and a plastic shatterproof bowl with no view of activity or natural light. Not that any light would actually penetrate the murky, dirty water that our poor scaly friend has been swimming in. It's heartless we tell you. Just heartless. Here you give baby Jane a relaxing lavender bath if she gets even the faintest smudge of dirt, but you let your poor goldfish swim in his own excrement for weeks. And have you seen the size of one of his poops?

The Golden Doodle

Before the kids arrived you used to dote on your dog. You'd take him to the dog park, rub his belly all day, and if you lived in a major metropolis, push him around in a stroller and dress him in designer clothes you got at Bark, Bath, and Beyond. But then you had kids, and the poor dog went from king of the castle to disregarded doormat. You'll sit and give your baby "pressure point" colic massages, but the last time you actually touched your poor hound was to push him away from the bouncy seat. And you let your preschooler change his name to Pretty Princess. No wonder he chews their toys. No wonder he raises his leg and tries to declare ownership of the crib, the couch, and the baby activity mat. He wants something to call his own. He wants justice, and belly rubs, and more peanut butter treats. Oh, and one more thing. He wants clean water every day so he won't have to drink from the toilet bowl anymore. Even Golden Doodles need some respect.

Maybe this was enough of a wake-up call for you. Maybe you're already outside playing tug-of-war with Pretty Princess or throwing an extra squirt of Miracle-Gro in the old watering can for the angry ficus. We're sorry we had to be the one to deliver such nasty mail, but someone's gotta stand up for the little guys. And someone's gotta stand up *to* the other little guys as well.

Meals on Wheels

We're not referring to the Good Samaritan delivery of meals to the less fortunate, the elderly, and the ill. We are referring to the mother who will do anything to get her child to eat a healthy meal, including pretend she is a drive-thru restaurant and let her child "park" and eat dinner on his LeapFrog See and Learn Alphabet Train. The Stay-at-Home Martyr has allowed the preparation of meals to turn into the most painful, elaborate, and time-consuming activity.

She's turned what was once a gourmet kitchen into a damn preschool. Her subzero fridge is now completely decorated with magnetic alphabet letters and artwork. Her honed, imported, slate tile floor has been completely covered by gingham oilcloth for ongoing art workshops. And her kitchen drawers (which now require serious dexterity to open) are stocked with baby food grinders, baby food strainers, baby food cube freezer trays with lids, stackable snack cups, spill-proof snack cups, drink cups, travel cups, travel cups with straws, spill-proof travel cups with straws, travel spoons and forks, metal spoons and forks with rubber grips, drink box holders, travel drink box holders, bottles, travel bottles, bottle liners, bisphenol-A–free plastic bottles, glass bottles, shatterproof plates, suction plates, three-portion divided suction plates, and five-portion divided suction travel plates with lids. And that's not including any of the actual food.

She's equally crazy about getting her fussy child to eat. She's famous for her "bugs on a log," she's cut fruit into tiny garden flowers, built tantalizing forests of broccoli, and scraped some eyes and a smile off a piece of bread so her kid could have "Tubby Toast" breakfast. She's put green food coloring in eggs with a side of ham (okay, turkey bacon but don't tell little Griffin) and used spaghetti sauce as a vehicle to hide numerous pulverized vegetables. She will do anything and will spend any amount of time in order to cook things the way her picky kids require.

First of all, your children can't "require" anything of you. They are subordinates. They are barnacles on the boat of life. You like to *think* they require it of you, so that you have an excuse for not exercising, showering, etc., etc., etc. But a child doesn't actually *need* a waffle with an imprint of a Disney character like he leads you to believe. Second of all, kids like quesadillas. They also like hot dogs. And they usually like PB&J. Throw in an apple, or hell, even applesauce counts as fruit, and you've just saved yourself forty minutes of meal prep time that you can now apply toward exercise or your newfound hobby. If you are the type of mother who simply must prepare a hearty meal with veggies, meats, and grains, the slow cooker is your new best friend. We know the idea of it conjures up images of chili cook-offs, old ladies, and that family with eighteen children whose names all start with "J," but we guarantee you will be happy if you plug that bitch in and let dinner cook itself.

Here are three basic recipes that our families probably see more often than they'd like to on the dinner table. They all require four steps a seventeen-month-old could follow. 1) Turn on the machine. 2) Throw in the meat. 3) Throw in the sauce. 4) Cover. 5) Enjoy!

Garland's Aloha Chicken

Turn on the machine.
Throw in some chicken breasts.
Throw in barbecue sauce mixed with crushed pineapple.
Cover and cook for eight hours.

Pam's "Impress the Boss" Cream of Mushroom Chicken

Turn on the machine.
Throw in some chicken breasts.
Throw in some cream of mushroom soup.
Cover and cook for eight hours.

Grandma Esther's Sunday Brisket

Turn on the machine.
Throw in some brisket.
Throw in Lipton Onion Soup mix with water.
Cover and cook for eight hours.

Germs Are Good (and Other Reasons to Stop Cleaning Your House)

We've all heard about the medical community's fear of overusing antibiotics and creating uber-bacteria resistant to even the biggest and baddest heavyweight meds on the pharmacy shelf. Along the same lines, household germs are likely mutating and gaining force with every spritz of the Lysol can we release. Sure, no one wants *E. coli* or Staphylococcus, but no one wants a germ that will take over the world either. Besides, there have been numerous studies done that prove a child who grows up around more dirt, pet hair, and even germs has a greater immune system and far fewer allergies than one who doesn't. That's our excuse for only doing minimal cleaning, and we're sticking with it!

Another way to fight the development of these uber-germs is to stop religiously scrubbing the floors, counters, doorknobs, toilets, sinks, etc. It's good to be neat. It's good to keep things relatively organized. But we know a few women who vacuum twice a day. Who scrub their bathrooms a couple times a week. Who actually make their beds every day and don't just pull the covers up and pretend like it's made! Who IRON!!!

Since housekeeping is a slippery slope (really, who can really empty just one trash can? Or wipe down one counter and not the other?), here are some basic guidelines for maximizing free time. The goal here is not to turn your house into a germ-ridden pigsty, but rather free up just enough time in your day for you to implement all that we discussed way back in Chapter Three. Remember getting a life and all that?

Goodwill Means Goodbye

We know you never want to forget the first bottle little Jaime sucked from. And that bassinet is the closest thing you still have of those precious newborn days. The first board book, the first bathing suit with ruffles on the butt, the first indoor basketball hoop, the first tricycle, the first soccer cleats, the first American President posterboard report, the first prom dress. The "firsts" never stop, and as beautiful as they are, as a group they're not quite so lovely. They're junk. Piles of extraneous "things" that fill your garage, your cabinets, under your beds, and ultimately your mind. This junk makes it almost impossible to have a stress-free house because it all needs to be cleaned, organized, and stored. So start purging!

As painful as it is, it's time to fill some Hefty bags and share the wealth. Don't do it when your kids are home or when you are especially hormonal. Every item you shove in that bag will suddenly become your child's "favorite thing EVER!" And doing it while PMS-ing will be worse than making yourself sit through a double feature of *Sophie's Choice* and *Terms of Endearment*.

> After all, they're just things. The real memorabilia from your children's lives has settled safely in your heart and in theirs.

Of course you're going to want to hold on to the special things. One idea is to keep a giant Rubbermaid box for each of your children. It contains special things they've made or received over the years. They love looking through it and commenting on how "lame" you are for saving stuff. And yet they keep going back to read the same notes, the same poems, the same silly pictures, year after year.

We guarantee that if you fill those Hefty bags and deliver them to pretty much anyone who will take them, you will feel a great sense of relief. Your home will lighten with your mood. After all, they're just things. The real memorabilia from your children's lives has settled safely in your heart and in theirs.

Kids Are Maid to Help

When it comes to cleaning, you don't have to do it alone. And you shouldn't. Although it will take infinitely longer to have your kids help you clean at first, in the long run, these little tykes can learn to be great helpers. Besides, unless you've given birth to members of the royal family, children need to learn responsibility and know that you're not going to be their servant. Not only should they put away their own stuff, but they should have regular tasks to do around the house.

Granted, they're not going to like it in the beginning and will fight you tooth and nail. You can try to make everything into a game (cleanup basketball is a good one, but somewhere down the line, your kid will wise up and realize that cleaning up inherently sucks). To help things along, here are some tricks. First, don't call housework "chores." It makes it sound automatically unappealing. You could say, "Honey, I need you to do a chore for me. Run over to the pantry and eat everything sugary you can find." Sadly, your child would be whining so loudly after hearing the word "chore," he would have missed the entire second part of the task. Instead try some creative re-naming (see our fourth point below).

Second, don't threaten kids with having to "help" Mommy. Kids should help Mommy whenever she needs help. It shouldn't be some horrible thing children have to do when they've misbehaved. We hear people do this all the time. "If you don't stop spitting down your sister's shirt, you are going to spend the day helping Mommy." (Still using the third person, too.) How about a real threat? A "natural consequence." "If you spit one more time down your sister's shirt, you're going to spend

> Don't threaten kids with having to "help" Mommy. Kids should help Mommy whenever she needs help. It shouldn't be some horrible thing children have to do when they've misbehaved.

the whole weekend writing a research paper on what organisms exist in human saliva!"

Third, don't feel guilty about asking your kids to help around the house. As a parent, you have every right to just tell your kids to put down whatever they're doing and complete whatever task you're asking them to do. NOW! The down side of this approach is that it may lead to a life of conflict, frustration, nagging, and poor family relations. Forcing them or making housework a punishment is like sending the dog to their crate when they're in trouble. They begin to associate it with bad feelings and overall negativity.

Fourth, give the chore a fun name. When our friend Susan's kids were little, their friends told them to NEVER go on the "Haunted Mansion" or "Pirates of the Caribbean" rides at Disneyland because they were WAY too scary. So when she finally agreed to suck it up and join the sea of sweaty, pasty, thrill-seeking tourists, her kids were already dead set against going on any ride they couldn't actually see from the line. Determined to get her $300 worth of entrance fees, she decided to do some creative name fabrication. She asked them if they were interested in going on "Barges of the Bayou" or maybe "The Colonial Funhouse."

They looked at her skeptically. "Is that sort of like the pirate one or the haunted one?"

She chuckled. "No, silly goose, it's like a barge on a bayou and an old Colonial house full of fun." They reluctantly agreed and wound up loving every minute of it. Especially the dark, steep hill and the goofy ghost guys that hitched a ride on their laps.

As far as housework goes, the same rule applies. Tape a damn Swiffer refill cloth to the bottoms of the kids' shoes and tell them to go play "Blades of Glory Championship Ice Skating Slide Race." (We've found that our kids are more impressed and enticed by long, extravagant game names.) We can't take full credit; Mary Poppins did it first with her brilliant game of "Tidy Up the Nursery" and "Snap, the Job's a Game." Other enticing house-cleaning games could include:

• Scat-Tracker's Adventure Hunt — Go clean up the dog poo.

• Supersonic Textile Origami Playoffs — Go fold the laundry.

• Colossal Confusing Geometric Kitchen Puzzle — Go load the dishwasher.

• Aquaman Undersea Total Submersion Tactic — Go take a bath.

Remember, it's all in the presentation.

We're sure by now you wish the lecturing, the criticizing, and all the "do this, change that" could end right here. Or maybe six and a half chapters ago. Sorry. We must press on. The exponential effect of your Martyring has not stopped at the doors of your household. It has seeped out and infiltrated the relationships you have with friends and family members. If you hope to retain or regrow some form of extended support and love, there's another group of living creatures you must address.

Chapter Eight

The Friends and Family Plan of Attack

When you were single, you clung tightly to your single BFFs while sipping trendy cocktails at hip, overcrowded bars. You plowed through designer discount racks as a competitive team and sat all night listening to boyfriend voice messages to dissect the meaning of each and every syllable. When you got married, you encircled yourself with married BFFs, swapped "pistachio-crusted protein" recipes, meddling in-law stories, and various ways to pre-treat skid marks. Now that you're a Stay-at-Home Martyr, your fave five on your speed dial includes your new fellow martyr BFFs, your pediatrician, and your lactation consultant's cell number. Let's take a look at how your life has changed over the years:

	Still Single	Just Married	Now Martyr
#1 conversation:	Your latest boy-toy	Your husband	Your kid
#1 restaurant is:	Trendy	Romantic	Kid-friendly
#1 medical visit:	Free clinic	Gyno	Urgent care
#1 fantasy:	He'd propose	He'd get you pregnant	He'd leave you alone

Now that you're a Martyr, your focus has changed. You have tunnel vision when it comes to your old life and can't see the forest through your kids. Especially not a "forest" that includes your friends and family members. It's a rare occurrence that you venture outside of your circle of Martyr cohorts, and if you ever do, it's out of obligation rather than desire. You call your old college roommate on her birthday to wish her well. You pack up the kids and go to your cousin's wedding (and if the kids aren't invited, you say screw her and vow to never send her a holiday photo card again). As time goes on, even those events get fewer and farther between. Gone are the dozen phone calls a day to your single friends and the married ones without children. These days your "in case of emergency" people are your enclave of preschool moms, park friends, and Mommy-and-Me group members who support you better than the top-of-the-line Bravado nursing bra.

Sure, your Martyr pals are great to have on hand when you can't remember the correct swaddle sequence of the Miracle Blanket . . . but there are plenty of good reasons why you need other people in your life as well.

You may not see this as much of a problem. Right now you don't need or want anyone in your life who doesn't understand your obsession with your children. You're way too busy with "bath time," "music time," and "Impressionist masters time" to hear about your old friends' self-centered problems like a broken engagement or a boss who's sexually harassing them. (What the hell's she complaining about? It must be nice to have *someone* attracted to you!) So you keep your non-Martyrs at bay, screening their calls and ignoring their e-mails until they finally get the message. Believe me, it's a mutual standoff since they too are tired of hearing you go on ad nauseum about your son's "terrible second grade math score and how it's going to affect his chances of getting into a good private school and hence a top college where he deserves to be since he enjoys the finer things in life and that it's your job to push him since your parents didn't push you and who knows where you would be right now if they had!" (We nodded off just writing the damn thing.)

But believe us, you'll find that distancing yourself from your old friends and relatives will only backfire in the end. Like they say, make new friends but keep the old, one is silver and the other really comes in handy when the shit hits the fan. Sure, your Martyr pals are great to have on hand when you can't remember the correct swaddle sequence of the Miracle Blanket, and both you and your baby are about to lose your shit. But there are plenty of good reasons why you need other people in your life as well, especially those you had before you pushed out your cute little tax deduction.

If You Don't Have Something Nice to Say . . . You Must Be a Martyr

You buy your kids things like dark-skinned, anatomically correct baby dolls and C.E.O. Barbies. You teach them about nondiscrimination, equality, and how it's okay for two men to love each other more than as just friends despite your own closemindedness. And yet you yourself are so competitive and judgmental. Uh-huh, yes you are. You compare and contrast every aspect of other women's children with your own, whether it be whose is the first to walk, go poo-poo in the potty, or get into the better preschool. As soon as a child is born, a new mom tallies everything from their Apgar score to their IQ score and checks it against their peers. Moms say they just want their children to be happy, but what they really mean is that they'll only be happy when they do better than everyone else.

We moms also pick apart other mothers' parenting methods, especially if they don't fall in the Martyr spectrum. If another woman isn't as self-sacrificing, doting, or life-abandoning as you are, she's pointed out by you and your buddies and attacked like lions on a zebra carcass. "Can you believe she's so selfish she hires a nanny so that she can go to the gym three days a week?" "I heard she went away with her husband for the entire weekend and abandoned her kids with a sitter! (Gasp!) That wasn't a blood relative! (Double gasp!)" Or "Look at her reading a book while her kid sits on that swing begging to be pushed! And it's not even a parenting book!" (Triple gasp! Someone call child protective services!)

We all know how powerful the green-headed monster of envy can be. We all went to high school and wanted better boyfriends, better clothes, and better class C narcotics. We know how competitive, critical, and nasty girls can be to each other, and how good that surge of pride feels after cutting down a lesser specimen. "Hasn't she ever heard of a *bra?*" "I've only seen that kind of makeup in drag shows." "Gawd, I'd never smile if I was as dentally challenged as her." And now that we're all grown up and have kids of our own, our competitive skills are so sharp we could use them to engrave jewelry. And we use them every chance we get to make ourselves feel superior.

What's wrong with us?! Instead of appreciating the effort this woman puts into keeping herself attractive and healthy, we hate her for it. Instead of rooting for ourselves, we root against her. It's much easier to be lazy and run-down and call anyone who gives a shit what they look like "vain" or "bitch." And any good Martyr would rather die than have her child be the last one to walk, talk, or grasp the quadratic formula, and take home the bronze in the Martyr Olympics.

Why not turn all that destructive energy on yourself and get motivated? It's been six months since you weaned, and you're still wearing that stretched-out nursing bra. Go splurge on a pricey matching bra and panty set. And check out your legs. There's nothing "itsy-bitsy" about those spider veins. Get yourself to a dermatologist and have them exterminated. Stop putting others down and prop yourself up by treating yourself to something stress relieving. Maybe a eucalyptus salt glow massage, or hire Marco the attractive personal trainer to spot your squats. What?! It's all in the name of good health and self-preservation. And if you just have to talk trash about *someone*, there's always the mother-in-law (or join your local PTA, where you will inevitably find plenty of women far more deserving of your frustration).

It takes two to compete. And if you keep your trap closed and drop out of the race, it won't take long before you notice a newfound sense of peace. And once the constant inner chatter of competitive mothering is gone, you'll realize you have enough free time and mental space to actually do something for yourself. Oh, and you should also notice that the kid whose mother wouldn't push him on the swing has taught himself how to pump. He's smiling with pride, yelling, "Mommy, look at me! I did it all by myself!" And she's smiling right back at him and shooting him a thumbs-up!

> Once the constant inner chatter of competitive mothering is gone, you'll realize you have enough free time and mental space to actually do something for yourself.

Martyrs Have a Short Shelf Life

Although right now you couldn't imagine a life without your Martyr friends in it, there will come a day when you'll drift apart. Time marches on. Families move. Kids change schools and wind instrument classes. Without your kids in the same class or after-school activity, you'll grasp at straws to hold onto, desperate to find something you still have in common. "Oh, Justin is about to get his first molars? Thank God, so is my Barron." I know you're

surprised, but if you think about it, do these women really enrich your life, and you theirs? Ask yourself these questions:

- Do I really like these women all that much, or do I overlook their faults because I need them so much in my life right now?

- Are my Martyr friends genuinely interested in hearing about the tantrum my kid threw because he couldn't deal with the seams in his socks, or are they just waiting for me to stop venting so they can chime in and vent about their own kids?

- How long can I converse about a topic other than my children before I have nothing left to say?

- Would I really enjoy these people's company if we weren't talking about every detail of our children's mishaps, frustrations, or achievements?

Some of these women may turn out to be genuine friends. Friends who are willing and capable of expanding the friendship to include things other than baby BMs and sleep schedules. These are the ones to hold on to. But a good majority of these women are only interested in having someone to bitch to and to express their undying adoration for their children to. These are the ones who must go. These are the ones who are denying you the time to cultivate any interest or hobby. Every forward step you try to take out of their messed-up world, they will pull you back with guilt and manipulation. This is why you must be wary of the insidious Martyr-Martyr dynamic. If you decide to spend a morning at the gym instead of the PTA book fair, believe me, you will be targeted like the moms you once tore apart with them.

Now that you see what can go wrong in this type of relationship, you may be wondering who else is out there. The most obvious choice is the guy you agreed to spend the rest of your life with. As previously discussed, tired, busy mommies mistakenly rely on their husbands for contact with the outside world and much-needed emotional support. It never works. Since he's always the one with the "you won't believe what happened today . . ." story, it only builds resentment and a greater sense of loneliness for Mommy. Here are some fundamental reasons why your husband can't be the one to fill all your gaps.

Husbands Can't Share Lip Gloss

You've heard it said that men are from Mars and women from Venus, and while it makes for one heck of a catchy book title, it also happens to be very true. Men are so different from women that it does often feel like we are dealing with a different species altogether. Any female can attest to the fact that there are aspects of the male gender that she will never comprehend. Never in our wildest dreams could we imagine doing some of the asinine things they do, such as:

· Paint their faces in their favorite sports team colors, don rainbow wigs, and yell at a TV screen like idiots.

- Get up at 4:00 a.m. on a bitter cold morning, climb a tree with guns in their hands, and sit still for hours waiting for an innocent deer to come close enough to blast its freakin' head off.

- Go completely ga-ga at the slightest hint of girl-on-girl action.

Despite the few things that draw us together, there's an undeniable gap that exists between us. This is why you must keep gal pals at your side. They understand us better than anyone with a Y chromosome ever could, and we can say and do things with them that we could never say or do with our husbands. Like bitch about our husbands. As progressive as our men think they are (because they've managed to suppress their inner caveman and change a diaper or two), they would never want to have a lengthy discussion about wedges vs. kitten heels or the advantages of feminine protection with wings. They'd never be excited to see Diane Lane's latest "I've-moved-to-some-quaint-village-in-Europe-to-find-myself-and-have-reckless-sex-with-the-first-hot-foreigner-who-buys-me-a-café-au-lait" romantic comedy, or meet at the food court to enjoy a perfectly acceptable meal of a Cinnabon and Diet Coke.

> This is why you must keep gal pals at your side. They understand us better than anyone with a Y chromosome ever could.

Things You Should Never Invite Straight Men To:

· Home decor expo

· Sarah McLachlan concert featuring special guest Kylie Minogue

· Annual pap smear

· *The Notebook* book club discussion

· *The Nutcracker on Ice*

· Anything with Shirley MacLaine in it

· *The Vagina Monologues*

· Pretty much anything with vagina in the title that isn't porn

Yes, men are from Mars and we're from Venus, and this is yet another reason you need girlfriends who will send Uranus to Pluto when you won't quit obsessing about your kids. Here's another one . . .

Women Live Longer than Men

In all developed countries, women live longer than men. Sometimes this difference is as much as ten whole years! There are various thoughts as to why this is so. Some experts believe it has to do with evolution. Others say it's because of lifestyle. Although the reason we live longer may not be certain, it *is* certain that once our husbands start dropping off like flies, we'll be left with only our girlfriends and our kids to keep us company (and after reading the next chapter, you won't put much faith in your kids tripping over themselves to keep you company). So if you don't make an effort to keep your girlfriends, or if you don't have enough life insurance on your husband to reel in a young aspiring model/pool boy, you're destined for loneliness.

Here's another interesting statistic for you . . . married men live approximately ten years longer than single ones do. Unlike the other statistic, there's no mystery as to why this is true. We cook them healthy meals instead of them grabbing something on the way home that comes in a bucket. We also nag them to stop smoking, cut down their drinking, and force them to see a doctor on a regular basis. Women, however, live to be the same age whether they're married or not. We guess the life of a football widow and constantly having to clean the errant urine drops around the toilet rim don't add much in terms of life span. Who would have thunk it?

Granted, there'll be some frustrations when the retirement villages become fully loaded with females. It'll be difficult to find incontinence pads at the drugstores because of the strong demand, and if there's ever the anomaly of a single man in the community, women will flock to his townhouse with a tuna-noodle casserole and a "come hither" look (which, with dentures and cataracts, may also resemble a "come take me trick-or-treating look"). But for the most part, if we keep connected to our girlfriends, life will be fabulous. We won't have to wear thong underwear or fake orgasms anymore (just kidding, honey!). It will be one long girl's night out, and the pain of having to say good-bye to our husbands will be eased by the comforting arms of our fellow shopping, drinking, eating, wine-tasting, spa-frequenting female friends.

Divorce Happens to Half of Us

Just because you're married now doesn't mean that you're necessarily going to stay that way. Unless you're a devout Catholic or a member of the Osmond family besides Marie, you stand about a 50 percent chance of becoming an "ex." And when the settlement battles are over and your stalking behavior comes to an end, you'll be left with half your savings, your James Blunt CDs, and best of all, your girlfriends. And I don't mean your Martyr girlfriends.

At first, your Martyrs will pretend to be supportive. They'll offer to watch your kids if you need alone time or take you out for a drink whenever it's "his" night with the kids. But we all know that the Martyr won't leave her kids for a trip to the bathroom let alone a cocktail with a desperately-in-need friend. And by the time you've cut your loser husband's head out of all your family photos, your Martyrs will fade out of the picture as well. It's not that they don't care; it's that they now see you as a threat to their own stability. As much as they might complain about their husbands, they still want them around to change the air conditioner filter and fund their Baby Gap habit. And now that your new first priority will be finding a place to live or looking for a job, things like discussing the virtues of the new Dreft stain-stick may not hold the same allure they once did.

Whether you're the one to call it quits on the marriage, or your dirty-lying-no-good-rotten-bastard-husband, one thing is for sure: You'll need a shoulder to cry on. Without your Martyr friends to rely on to dry your tears and torch his car, you need your old girlfriends around more than ever. They've held your hand in the past through bad breakups, bad hair, and bad skin conditions. They've kept you company on Date Night Saturday and watched *When Harry Met Sally* with you for the umpteenth time reciting, "Waiter, there's too much pepper on my paprikash," with smushed-up faces. If you haven't burned too many bridges and forgotten too many birthdays, let your fingers do the walking and reconnect with your old friends.

Learn to Talk the Talk

Enough already. You get it. You've seen the error of your ways and agree that it's time to pick up the phone and call your non-Martyr peeps. But how do you take that first step? What are you going to say after so much time has passed? And what the hell are you going to talk about if not your children? If you're stymied to make scintillating conversation that doesn't revolve around your kid's newest feat or his sudden aversion to chicken tacos, here are some tips to guide you through the inevitable pregnant pauses of your first conversation. Whenever you're tempted to talk about your children, stop, take a beat, and think of something else to say. Here are some ideas:

When you're tempted to talk about:	Talk about this instead:
Your kid's mission project	Last night's missionary position
Your breastfeeding struggles	Your latest breast exam results
Dr. Sears' latest book	*Dr. 90210*'s latest tummy tuck
Your kid's ear infection	Your latest yeast infection (if you don't have one, just make it up. Women can discuss the perils of yeast for hours.)
What stupid thing your husband did	What stupid thing your husband did (okay, some things never change)

Make New Friends

As wonderful and nostalgic as it can be to reconnect with old friends, your social possibilities are not limited to people who knew you when Aqua Net dominated the top half of your head. There are many women out there eager to make a new friend, just as tired of their current companion pool as you are. The trick is going to be not falling into old habits. Calling an old buddy and practicing child omission was a good start. But making a new friend can be much harder than just tagging them and saying, "You're it," on the playground. Like a stammering twenty-two-year-old boy trying to win the affection of anything female, sometimes we simply don't know where to begin. Here are a few conversation starters to get your inner conversationalist going again.

At yoga class . . .

"Down dog? How 'bout 'why don't you lie that damn dog down and catch a few Zs?' That'd get me to come back next week. You want to get a full-fat latte after class?"

At the nail salon . . .

After almost definitely being laughed at by at least three nail ladies, and refusing the paraffin dip, gel tips, and beard wax, turn to the gal next to you who is trying to explain why neither "round" nor "square" will help her lose weight and say, "If we band together, we can bring them down. Laugh and point on three." If she follows your lead, you have a friend for life. If she cowers and continues to accept the abuse, she was never worthy to begin with.

Or: "Does this polish make my toes look fat?"

At the park . . .

"If the ice cream guy sold Jell-O shots, he'd make a fortune."

On the treadmill . . .

"I like the back row so I know no one is looking at my butt."

At church (doesn't matter which one) . . .

Ask the person next to you, not the one sleeping (she's very tired after having been up all night with a newborn and has joined the congregation for the free day care), to play hymnal golf.

Rules: When you're asked to open to a certain hymn or verse, set the par and see who can beat it by opening to the hymn with the least amount of page flipping. If a "hymn-in-one" is achieved, other players must buy winner a drink.

Family Matters

Just as it's important to keep your real friends close, it's a good idea to keep your family within arm's reach as well. Sure they bug the freakin' fudge out of you, but whether you actually enjoy spending time with them, or wish they'd tell you that you were adopted so things would finally make sense, this dysfunctional lot can actually provide a whole lot of support. And we don't just mean all that free babysitting, although that should be good enough reason on its own.

The Parent Trap

When you have a kid, many of your own parent/child issues come back with a vengeance. When you see your parents reenacting the same bad behaviors with your child that they did with you, the pain can flow back with the force of an overdue period. If you had a controlling mother, it may send you into a tizzy if she so much as comments on your daughter's mismatched socks. If your father was an absentee parent, it may send you through the roof when he shows up thirty minutes late to little Benjamin's birthday party. And since you're a Martyr who believes in protecting your young above all else, you'll want to keep your parents as far away as a snot-nosed kid at the park.

You need to get past this and move on. We know you think you're right and they are horrible grandparents, but things are usually more complex than that. Allow us to present a logical argument that might get you to at least question your motives. If you believe wholeheartedly that your parents were so awful and dysfunctional in raising you, then it would be fair to say that you are the product of unhealthy parenting. An obvious conclusion would then be that you, too, are f-ed up. From this, we could gather that your deciding who and when and how your family gets to interact with your child would also be coming from a place of dysfunction and unhealthy parenting. The natural conclusion to all of this is that *you are just as crazy as your parents were*.

The natural conclusion to all of this is that you are just as crazy as your parents were.

If you have it in you, get together with your parents and tell them how you feel. Give them a chance to defend themselves. Maybe they'll have good reasons for their bad behavior. Maybe their parents were even worse, and the dysfunction is being diluted across generations. Or perhaps you'll learn absolutely nothing about them except that they were lousy parents, but at least you'll finally get the stuff off your chest. Besides, now that you're a parent and see how trying it can be to raise kids, you may decide to forgive them and realize that they did the best job that they could, just like you're doing now.

PLUS, and this is an important plus, almost as important as the plus sign on a pregnancy stick, if you really want to do what's best for your child, you'll build a strong relationship with their grandparents. Grandparents are like regular parents filled with Twinkie cream. They're loving and protective but get to do all the good stuff like spoil people rotten and not discipline them, plus they get the added benefit of a good night's sleep. Sorry, but those are the rules. And unlike with you, your kids won't be affected by your parents' actions with the same strength you were. Only you can create those really deep scars on your kids, which you'll find out about twenty-some years from now when they have kids and want to keep you at a distance as well. Sorry, but again, those are the rules.

Sibling Rivalry

You and your siblings have a unique relationship. After years of growing up together under the same roof, you share a very special love for each other and a powerful bond. You have wonderful memories of them protecting you from school bullies, teaching you how to roller skate, and clueing you in on sexual terms that you wouldn't dare ask your parents about. And your kids will continue the tradition by protecting each other from online sexual predators, teaching each other how to use the Wii Rollerskating game, and clueing each other in on sexual terms that you've probably never heard of and would definitely never act out.

On the other hand, there's no one you hated more than your brothers and sisters because they knew just how to push your buttons. They knew your weak spots, your sensitivities, and where your embarrassing moles were. And they didn't think twice about using their arsenal to attack you whenever it suited their needs.

Now that you're all grown up with children of your own, you'd think you've grown past the sibling rivalry stuff. You're not as sensitive as you used to be, you've had all your moles removed, and you have cable so you feel pretty up to date on all the sexual terms. But if you're knee-deep in Mommy Martyrdom, the rivalry will continue going strong and will provide them with a whole new slew of material to work with.

If your siblings don't have any kids, they won't understand how you changed so drastically after popping one out. You used to go with the flow and now you go ape-shit when they hand your toddler a whole grape instead of cutting it up into miniscule pieces. They'll have a heyday with your Martyring ways from the get-go, starting with being forced to wear a sterile apron and mask before coming within twenty feet of your new baby.

If your siblings do have children but aren't Martyrs, they'll tease you unmercifully as well. They'll mock you when you allow your child to chuck his birthday cake across the table because he's simply expressing feelings of frustration. And *you'll* think they're the Queen of Mean when they demand their kids put away their toys without making it into a fun game or singing an accompanying cleanup song.

Unfortunately, if their relentless teasing makes you cut family ties, your kids will pay the biggest price. Aunts and uncles are really cool relatives to have because they teach the fun tricks like how to make fart sounds with your hand under your armpit, and they let you put on actual makeup instead of that cheap crap from Claire's. Plus, aunts and uncles are the door that leads them to the holy grail of family members: the cousins. Cousins have all the benefits of siblings without any of the rivalry stuff that makes them want to bash their heads in.

For the sake of your kids, don't let your Martyring ways get in the way of your relationship with your siblings. If there's more than one way to skin a cat (a theory we'll assume is true since no way in hell we're about to do research on it), there's more than one way to raise a kid. So ignore their teasing, cut them some slack, and don't take it all so seriously. You may even try to develop the ability to laugh at yourself. Even though you may not need them in your life right now, your kids do. And besides, they're going to really come in handy when your parents get old and smelly and need someone to give them sponge baths and change their adult diapers.

You're In (Law) for Trouble

This is a toughie. If you're one of the lucky ones, this section won't apply. But for the vast majority of women, their husband's mother thinks her darling son settled for an unworthy woman . . . you. Having a good relationship with your in-laws is like having a good relationship with irritable bowel syndrome. There's just nothing pleasant about either one, and you wish life could go back to what it was before the situation began. On the whole, your father-in-law isn't really the issue. You may have to tolerate the same "when I was your age" stories and a multitude of digestion-related body noises, but overall, he's benign.

It's the competitive, undermining, in-your-face, bloodsucking fiend, otherwise known as your mother-in-law, that's causing you all the grief. You two have had issues ever since you were brought home to "meet the parents." She smiled as she made pleasant conversation and drank her boxed wine, but you knew deep down she was thinking, "You little slut, having sex with my precious baby boy." At your wedding, she smiled as she complimented your gown, but you knew deep down she was thinking, "You little 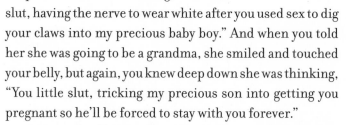 slut, having the nerve to wear white after you used sex to dig your claws into my precious baby boy." And when you told her she was going to be a grandma, she smiled and touched your belly, but again, you knew deep down she was thinking, "You little slut, tricking my precious son into getting you pregnant so he'll be forced to stay with you forever."

It's simple. She's jealous of the close relationship you get to have with her son. So she digs in at every opportunity. She criticizes your cooking. "Are you sure you've cooked that chicken long enough? I don't want to get sick *again*." She criticizes your housekeeping. "Looks like someone needs a new mop for their birthday." She criticizes your parenting. "I had all my children out of diapers well before their second birthday." Before you know it, she's dug so deep, you could crawl through the hole and have authentic spring rolls and Peking duck for dinner.

As bad as that typical mother-in-law/daughter-in-law scenario is, it's bumped up a notch when you're a Martyr and she won't go along with your Martyring ways. She refuses to stop giving little August a bottle even though you tell her the "experts" say it's time. She pooh-poohs your request to stop feeding baby Dylan more mashed peas after she's done because the "experts" say it'll lead to adolescent eating disorders. So you go all K-Fed on her ass and refuse unsupervised visits, which in turn causes stress in your marriage and hostility between the family.

We know you see this woman as dangerous as honey to a newborn, but relax. She really does have your children's best interests at heart. As long as she's not doing anything dangerous or neglectful, count your blessings (and the wad of cash you saved by not having to pay $15 to $20 an hour for a sitter!). We promise there will be no long-term damage done by a few extra bottles, a nauseating onslaught of hugs and lipsticky kisses, and some butt-ugly clothes she can't wait to see them wearing.

There are reasons beyond giving your children a sense of extended family to maintain these family relationships. Hopefully, it comes from actually loving the crazy lot and wanting to share life's joys and struggles together. If this approach is way too idealistic or downright ridiculous when discussing your family, then consider the fact that you will be more than likely spending your holidays, birthday parties, and vacations with these people. It's your attitude that will determine whether things go smoothly at Uncle Maury's Thanksgiving dinner, or if the to-go bags will be packed before the first pie's been cut.

Getting Away from It All (and Bringing It All with You)

Imagine this: a cool tropical setting, steel drums playing in the background, Tom Cruise look-alike juggling vodka bottles behind the bar, and then, total buzzkill . . . the Stay-at-Home Martyr comes barreling through like a rhino lugging a foldable crib, assorted beach chairs, a bag of sand toys, and a diaper bag large enough to pack up a kid going off to college. She's followed by her baby ducklings, who are prepared for any natural or man-made disaster. They're layered with sunscreen, wide-brim hats complete with wraparound neck flaps, and have flotation devices on every appendage. Incapable of relaxing, the Stay-at-Home Martyr watches her children like a hawk, prepared to spring into action and attack any hazard that comes their way.

Now doesn't that sound like a relaxing family vacation?! We sure hope so because that's what you can look forward to for the next umpteen years. When you're a Martyr, every aspect of your family vacation must revolve around your children. The location is dictated around their needs (a kid-friendly theme park and famous pancake restaurant is chosen over an idyllic lakeside getaway). The activities are scheduled around their interests (a train ride through the zoo with "Conductor Skippy" is picked over an afternoon of alternating naps and cocktails by the pool). And the meals are always eaten at a restaurant that offers crayons instead of a wine list. Your husband begs you to leave the kids with the hotel babysitter to get a brief respite and some much-needed alone time, but unless the sitter has a CPR certificate, a degree in child psychology, and studied under Dr. Spock himself, you'd never feel right about it. And maybe not even then.

> Tell your kids the plan for the day, which should include fun things for them, fun things for Daddy, and, although it goes against every cell in your Martyr-infested body, fun things for you as well.

The problem with this scenario (besides the obvious one of needing a vacation the moment you return home from one) is that it doesn't do any family member any good. You and your spouse are brain dead after days of mind-numbing kid things, and your kids still believe they are the center of the universe because you treat them like they are. A family vacation is just that, a vacation for the entire family. It's a give and take. A yin and yang. A compromise for all. You'd never dream of going on a family vacation and insist everyone watch you get a full-body massage, eat the garlic snails you crave at a fancy French bistro, and finish up the evening eating gourmet chocolates while watching *Friends* reruns in bed. So why should you indulge your kids in this manner?

Unless you and your husband enjoy spending your morning doing somersaults on the hotel lawn and an afternoon at the local Color Me Mine, take turns with activities. Tell your kids the plan for the day, which should include fun things for them, fun things for Daddy, and, although it goes against every cell in your Martyr-infested body, fun things for you as well. Then, and only then, can you call it a real family vacation and come home with lovely memories and souvenirs for everyone to enjoy through the years.

I'll Be Home for the Holidays (while the Rest of You Go Out and Have a Good Time)

Nothing says family like the holidays. Relatives gather together from across the globe to decorate a tree, eat their weight in chocolate Easter eggs, hide the matzoh, or help themselves to a third helping of turkey and stuffing.

Family reunions also happen under an endless umbrella of birthdays, weddings, graduations, funerals, and anniversaries. Under normal circumstances, being around family can be strained, but when you add in the Martyr factor, it can throw a wrench in the fire that's bigger than any found in a Craftsman tool set.

A Martyr finds family get-togethers to be a time of extreme tension, especially if the celebration isn't held under her roof where she isn't able to control the thousands of harmful influences that can and will contaminate her children. A relative's house may not be properly childproofed. There may be sharp ornaments on the lower branches of the Christmas tree that her kid could cut herself on, or fake snow cotton on the floor that she could pop into her curious young mouth and choke on. There may be a family dog that, for no apparent reason, decides to channel his inner dingo and eat her baby! Good God, you're one errant Easter egg away from being the breaking story on the evening news!

Even if the celebration *is* held at her home, there's one element that's guaranteed to freak her out: having other relatives' children around her own. These "wild animals" are raised without limits. They're allowed to watch noneducational television, leave their vegetables uneaten on their plate, and play games that encourage a winner (hence fostering low self-esteem in the ones who didn't). Having these hooligans around poses a negative threat on her tender young things. They might as well be handing them a speedball and a bong for Christ's sake.

Secretly, you criticize your relatives for being so lackadaisical with their children. Don't they know the repercussions of their actions? Haven't they read all of Elizabeth Pantley's proper parenting tips? These relatives are destined to raise a brood of craven wildebeests that even Supernanny couldn't tame. But did you know that these relatives are secretly criticizing you as well? You think you're being helpful when you advise them how to properly parent their children and share your wisdom about the perils of synthetic carpet and processed cheese. But they don't see it that way. They see you as arrogant and judgmental and think you're raising a brood of robotic weirdoes who don't even know the difference between Dora and Diego, or the rules to "Duck, Duck, Goose" because the game doesn't portray the behaviors found in nature (geese don't routinely chase ducks).

Whether you celebrate the holidays at your place, or have to drive to theirs, put away your Martyr instincts along with your fine jewelry and prescription medications that Uncle Harry will undoubtedly try to pocket. And remember, as hard as it is to endure a family celebration whenever it includes the actual family, it's still a hell of a lot better than having to get on a plane and travel to them.

Fly the Unfriendly Skies

Traveling to a distant relative's house puts a Martyr's stress level at Defcon Five. She's on high alert, attacking everyone in her path. From the time she leaves to the time she returns, it's a nonstop hellhole that she can't seem to climb out of. Nothing, and we mean nothing, is harder for a Martyr to endure than packing up her family and leaving the comforts of her sterilized, HEPA-filtered, cushioned-corners home. It's stressful enough just schlepping the endless paraphernalia that proper parenting entails, like elite strollers, special FDA-approved car seats, the stimulating but not overstimulating toys, and the full medical kit complete with ipecac for accidental poisoning and an anaphylactic pen in case a life-threatening allergy might develop mid-trip (a Martyr, like a true Girl Scout, is always prepared).

Once the plane takes off, it's mayhem at 35,000 feet as air pressure is neutralized by bottles and gum to prevent eardrum damage, a dizzying array of crayons and small toys are constantly picked up from the floor, crippling germs are wiped clean from armrests and folding trays, and an endless stream of non-sugary snacks is offered. After landing, it's off to the car rental to get the five-star safety-rated vehicle you reserved and confirmed three times, and then a drive to the hotel. There, the bottle heating/

sterilizing station is set up, and the foldable crib you lugged across the continent is assembled (the hotel crib could be covered in lead paint and have bars wide enough to pass a soda can through! No child would be safe!).

As bad as the hotel might be, it's still far better than staying at your relatives' home. There, you'll be frustrated that they won't kowtow to your baby's needs like you do at home. Activities won't be scheduled around his appointed nap times. And there won't be a no-walking, no-talking rule like at home, so he will be undoubtedly awoken by mumbling or floor creaks. It'll piss you off that they won't cater to your little schnookum's delicate palette by making him special meals. They raised their kids in the "if they're hungry enough, they'll eat anything" school and aren't about to change their rules now. And don't count on your relatives safety-proofing their home either since they raised their kids in the "oh, he won't stick his finger in the electric socket more than once" school and aren't about to change their rules about that, either.

Nothing, and we mean nothing, is harder for a Martyr to endure than packing up her family and leaving the comforts of her sterilized, HEPA-filtered, cushioned-corners home.

We know it's going to take all the inner strength you can muster, but when you decide to travel with children, you have to toss out your Martyr ways and go with the flow. If your kid doesn't take a nap at his regular time, so be it. If he doesn't eat a big meal, what the hell. Time will pass, life will go on, and worse things will happen. Your kid will wake up the next morning alive and well, and you might realize that a little flexibility, and a little less Martyring, may be just what the doctor ordered. Your child may discover he likes a new food, and you may discover that maybe, just maybe, a life without Martyring can be a great life indeed. And if that doesn't convince you, let's take a look at what's to come if you don't change your ways.

Chapter Nine

The Ghost of Martyr Future

You've seen your past and how your inner Martyr was born. You've seen your present and what happens to your life when you deny your own needs for the sake of your children. Now let's take the next step and journey into the not-so-distant future where you will feel the full brunt of your Martyring actions. As our last-ditch attempt to right what has gone so horribly wrong, we'll be your Ghost of Martyr Yet to Come. Just like the third ghost in the classic tale, *A Christmas Carol*, we'll hold a mirror up to your in-desperate-need-of-exfoliation face. Then you can see for yourself what your future holds once your own little Tiny Tim or Tina has grown old enough to go to full-day school, to sleep-away camp, to boy-girl parties, to graduation day, to their wedding day, and finally, to go forth and multiply. Then, and only then, can you decide if it was worth putting your children at the forefront of your life while shoving trivial things like your husband, your family, your friends, your career, and even your body to the back of your closet (with other crap you had no use for once you had kids, like your braless halter tops and crotchless panties).

Some moms actually look forward to their children getting older and becoming independent. They can't wait for a six-hour school day, drop-off playdates, and even (hold on tight) sleepovers with their friends! Having time apart from her kids is a time when a frazzled stay-at-home mom can finally restart her career, spend time alone with her spouse, and regain her identity (besides just being a giant Kleenex or trash receptacle to her kids).

But that's not the case for a Stay-at-Home Martyr. In fact, no matter how old her babies grow, or how independent they struggle to become, any good Stay-at-Home Martyr is always hard at work, hovering and controlling and making sure her children are properly cared for in the manner she dictates. She doesn't care how much she has to sacrifice to do her job; as long as she has her hooks deep within the souls of her children, she is happy. But her future is not bright. In fact, it's so dark and dreary that, like Ebenezer Scrooge, just catching a glimpse of it may send her into a frenzied state of fear and make her change her ways. On that note, set your little one down next to his VectorSphere, take our hands, and let's get a sneak peek at what you can look forward to.

School Daze

Granted, every parent cries a few tears when she sends her children off to kindergarten, but the true Martyr will cry a veritable river. Not only because she's emotional about her little baby growing up, and of course worried sick that he'll pick up a nasty germ since she's not able to Lysol the room down like a Silkwood shower, but also because she's panicked about all her newfound free time. What will become of her if she doesn't have little Alexandra to cater to 24/7? Idle hands may be the devil's workshop, but to a Martyr they're a one-way ticket to a three-refill vial of Xanax.

After an endless stream of reasons not to send junior to kindergarten until he's sprouting hair in private places, the day will finally come. Fear not, my dear Martyr, packing a sushi lunch and sending your little one off to elementary school does not mean giving up your days as a Martyr. In fact, schools offer a wide range of activities to keep you busy from drop-off to pickup, such as being a room parent, heading the fund-raising committee, assisting in the science center, being a class volunteer, and driving to and from every field trip. (Really, what kind of mother would allow her precious child to drive with a total stranger anyway?) Yes, schools are a mecca of Martyr opportunities. The school will get some cheap labor and you'll be close to your child to make sure his sweater is fully buttoned and his shoelaces properly double-knotted.

As your kids grow older, you may even consider homeschooling your children. What a perfect fit! You get to spend all day obsessing over your kids and keeping them away from negative influences that plague our schools like bad teachers, teenage smoking, illegal drugs, and sexual contact. Sure, they'll hate you and have no kids their age to spend time with, besides a few errant cousins or their imaginary friend, Scooter. But at least you'll be able to make sure that every minute of every day, your children are protected from harm, exposed to nurturing influences, and far away from things you frown upon like smoking, drugs, and (as your husband can attest to) sexual contact.

Plus, don't forget about the barrage of after-school activities that will have you racing all over town like a criminal in a high-speed police pursuit. What Martyr would deny the fruit of her loins the overwhelming assortment of lessons and classes and activities to choose from? A childhood without oboe lessons, gourmet cooking, drama club, Japanese class, and cotillion is no childhood for your little prodigy. Then, after the sun has set and the last coach has been reprimanded for not letting your kid play in the game as much as you feel he deserves, it's home to make a nutritious dinner with representatives of all major food groups, oversee the mountain of homework, and tuck your kids in for a full night's rest. Phew! A Martyr's work is never done!

Yes, if you continue your Martyring ways throughout your child's educational experience, you can expect to become even more isolated, more exhausted, have no outside interests, build more distance between you and your spouse, and have a mind, body, and soul that's so neglected, you don't even recognize yourself in your pre-baby pictures. And for what? Oh yeah. For your children of course. You did it all for the sake of your children. But unlike when your kids were small and didn't have much awareness of the world around them, they've grown old enough to realize that not all mothers share your same approach. They've seen some moms who actually allow their kids to stay up past their bedtime on weekends, eat raw cookie dough despite the risk of salmonella poisoning, and watch channels besides PBS! With their new awareness comes a level of mother/child resentment that rivals that of any James Dean movie, and your relationship with your teenagers will be one of constant give and take. You giving them everything they want to bribe them into loving you, and them taking the car keys without your permission to punish you for not letting them see a PG-13 movie like all the other kids because you fear they might hear someone say "hell" or "damn." Yup. Those will be good times.

The Ins and Outs of Offspring

You've spent the last eighteen years giving up your life for the sake of your children. You've given them everything they could possibly want or need, whether you could afford it or not. You've shielded them from harm and patiently explained to them why their actions weren't "appropriate" without any consequence or discipline. Now, despite your wishes to the contrary, your kids are finally grown up and ready to fly the coop. But what kind of children have you raised? Perfect children who are smart, confident, and kind? Maybe . . . maybe not. There are actually three distinct personality types of children that spawn from a true Stay-at-Home Martyr. Here's a description of those three children ranked by the strength of their invisible umbilical cord:

1. **A Petrified Cord:** This is a kid whose umbilical cord is so strongly attached to his Martyr after so many years, that it's actually petrified like a giant redwood. This type

of offspring doesn't have the fortitude to leave the house without the comforting shield of Mommy. The thought of going out into the big scary world without her hand to hold or her boo-boo bunny to ease his pain terrifies him. You've told your children so many times to "be careful" and "don't talk to strangers" that they can barely step foot out the door now that they're grown. After so many years of being protected, they're ill-equipped to deal with the outside world. Not only do they lack the backbone to do so, but emotionally, they lack the strength since no one thinks they're as special as they've been told all these years. If they ever do find a job, they expect their boss to praise their every task and say, "Good job!" after filing a paper correctly or giving a customer the right change. And when they don't get the accolades they require, they quit, move back home, and possibly never ever leave.

2. **The Spring-Loaded Cord:** This is the kid who can leave for a bit but then has to rush home for safety. He'll go to a local college and live in a crowded dorm but will return every weekend on the pretense of having (Mom do his) laundry or missing a home-cooked meal. Later, he'll graduate from school and get his own apartment, but he must share it with ten other people because of his deep-seated fear of being alone (caused by the fact you played with him every second of his life). He'll be able to get and hold a job, and unlike the petrified cord kid, he'll

even find love and get married one day. Unfortunately it won't last very long due to the fact that this mama's boy will insist that you come along on the honeymoon.

3. **A Severed Cord:** If your kid is very, very lucky, they'll emerge relatively unscathed after being raised by a Martyr. It doesn't happen very often. It occurs with about the same frequency as an inner city kid growing up to become a successful doctor or lawyer. We don't know how it happens really. Maybe rebellion. Maybe a mutant gene. But somehow, there are a few lucky children who are able to slip through the cracks and become completely independent adults. They can go to school out of state, move into their own apartment, get a good job, and have a steady relationship. And they don't feel the need to check in with their mommies every hour on the hour. In fact, they often move as far, far away from Mom as possible, maybe even to some formerly Nazi-occupied country. Unless their moms "sprechen sie deutsch," they don't even speak to them very often. (Which is fine with them because they'd rather spend their time raising the "rufenkegel" at Oktoberfest with Olga Van Lederhosen, the new woman in their life.)

Empty Nest = Empty Life

If you've raised a kid with either a spring-loaded or severed cord, it was bound to happen. The day you've feared since you pushed out your placenta. The day when your kid finally packs up her designer duds, her Egyptian cotton sheets, and her Sonicare Elite 9500 toothbrush (any Martyr knows the importance of good oral hygiene) and moves away from home. As her baby steps foot out of the house, she crumbles like good aged Roquefort.

It's called the empty nest syndrome, a time when a Martyr gets her life back and doesn't know what to do with herself. Believe it or not, some mothers actually celebrate this time. After years of being hindered by little ones underfoot, they're finally able to talk like a truck driver in rush-hour traffic, make loud passionate love in every room of the house (with good lighting), enjoy a good HBO marathon on surround sound, and travel without fear that the teenagers will turn their home into an opium den for sex-crazed adolescents.

But if you, dear Martyr, haven't remedied your ways, there'll be nothing to celebrate when this big day arrives. With your children out of the house, you have nothing to focus on. And with nothing to focus on, you spin out of control. Your life loses all meaning and, like your nest, you too become empty. Now you and this guy you barely recognize anymore (but continue to keep furnished in deodorant and clean socks) rattle around in a home devoid of children.

What will you do without a child to dote on? How can you survive if you don't know your kids are eating properly and getting enough sleep? How will you start your morning without organizing a frantic schedule or end it without performing live puppet theater bedtime performances of Eric Carle's *The Very Hungry Caterpillar*? A world without a child to obsess about is no world for you. No how. No way.

These days, instead of busying yourself around the clock quizzing your child on irregular French verbs or hand-sieving tomato sauce so there aren't any yucky lumps in it, your schedule is wide open. Here's a look at how you fill up your day:

6:45 a.m. You wake up. You try to sleep in but after so many years of waking up before your children to draw maple syrup happy faces on their homemade whole-grain pancakes before they leave for school, it's hard to reset your inner clock.

8:30 a.m. You say goodbye to your husband as he leaves for the office. It's one of the few words you'll speak to him the whole day.

8:45 a.m. You watch home movies of your children before they committed the ultimate sin of leaving you, and you cry.

9:00 a.m. You wander through your kids' rooms, which you keep like a shrine. Your husband suggested turning them into a gym or home office, but you're adamantly opposed to the idea, convinced that one day, they'll see the error of their ways and return home.

10:00 a.m. You think up an excuse and call your kids. No answer. You leave a message.

11:00 a.m. You go to a computer store and buy mommy/child web cameras.

1:00 p.m. Home for lunch. You grab a pizza Lunchables and stack of Pringles. You're so used to making meals only for your children you've grown quite fond of the stuff.

2:00 p.m. No word back from your kids. You call them again. This time you lay on the guilt.

2:19 p.m. You drive through the old elementary school pickup line just for old time's sake.

3:00 p.m. You meet an old Martyr pal for coffee. You watch a young mother with her small children and criticize her parenting skills.

6:00 p.m. You and your husband eat dinner in separate rooms. You in your kid's room, smelling their pillows; him by the computer, playing cyber poker and secretly logging onto his account on dirtypanties.com.

6:30 p.m. The kids finally call back. You are happy. They quickly answer your barrage of questions, then tell you that the doorbell is ringing, there's someone on the other line, they were just stepping out, or the battery on their cell phone is dying. On some level you realize they just want to get off the phone, but you don't let yourself think about that.

6:45 p.m. You go to Radio Shack to buy them a new cell phone battery.

Sound like a fun day? Let's hope so because if you stay on this track, it can all be yours. Go ahead. Try to deny it and say you'll be different. You'll be fine when your kids leave. You may even go back to work. Okay. Let's ponder that for a bit.

Back to the Workforce

With your days as free as Nelson Mandela, you may want to jump-start your career. We know it's been a long time since you punched the ol' time clock, but it just may be the perfect opportunity to get back in the game. Before you got pregnant, you had a rewarding job and were actually quite good at it. You even had fun. You gossiped with coworkers, enjoyed your assignments, and Xeroxed your body parts during holiday office parties. Yeah, you kind of miss going to an office. But after so many years out of the rat race, what are you possibly qualified to do? Fortunately, you've actually gained a lot of experience being a Stay-at-Home Martyr, which can now open up a lot of doors. Here's a partial list of opportunities that you're now more than qualified to tackle:

- **Work for the Consumer Product Safety Commission.** With your vast knowledge of recalled toys and child safety regulations, you'd get that corner office with a view in no time.

- **Health Protection Agency.** You're up to date on all the latest health concerns like microwaving food in plastic containers or the perils of cooking in scratched Teflon pans.

- **Lead a Montessori Mommy-and-Me group.** With your superior parenting techniques, it'd be a crime not to educate others in your child-rearing methods.

- **Work for a company that makes GPS systems.** With your comprehensive awareness of road conditions and traffic patterns gained from driving three children to various schools, orthodontists, pediatricians, and lessons, you know all the tricks to maneuver around a busy city.

- **Air traffic controller.** After years of scheduling and organizing field trips, after-school activities and play-dates, overseeing a few jumbo jets should be a breeze.

My Martyr, My Pimp

Whether you go back to work or not, your main job will always be to care for your children. But now, instead of being obsessed with things like exposing them to culture and making sure they're slathered with sunscreen, you've fixated on keeping them from settling down with the wrong person. And as much as you wish they would stay single for as long as possible (and stay focused on the two most important things in life—their future and their mother), there's just no stopping the power of the hormone.

Therefore, you take it upon yourself to become their personal matchmaker. It's ironic because when they lived with you, you did everything you could to keep your children from having s-e-x. You'd enforce curfews. You'd instill an open-door policy whenever they had a guest over of the opposite sex. You role-modeled abstinence. And you'd find that old baby monitor and hide it in their room so you could eavesdrop on their personal phone conversations. (We know you're making a mental note of that idea for later.)

But now that your kids are all grown up, you're obsessed with sparing them a life of marital misery and have devoted yourself to finding them a suitable mate. You fix them up with every Tom, Dick, or Harriet you come across that has a fine leather briefcase, a nice watch, or is dressed in hospital scrubs. And watch out, if you happen to spot a man taking his elderly grandmother out to lunch, you'll have his cell, home, and office numbers before Granny can gum her first spoonful of turkey chili and corn bread.

When it comes to love, you do what you do best: push.

As much as your kids protest, you can't sit idly by and watch them flounder through relationships with girls named "Bliss" and guys with a passion for motocross. Once again, they don't know what's good for them. They don't have your wisdom. They don't know what's really important in a mate. They think it's about silly things like smokin' hot looks and sexual chemistry. But you know better. For your daughters, it's a man who can fix things around the house, has a well-paying job, and is close to his mother. For your son, it's a woman who loves to clean, is a culinary whiz, and has ample breeding hips (and insists that his mother live with them).

When it comes to love, you do what you do best: push. You push to keep them single as long as you can, and then when you realize you can't force them to finish their education via satellite from a deserted island (well, deserted except for you), you push them to hook up with someone you've chosen (or have at least approved of).

At some point, though, you realize that their biological clock is winding down to a slow tick (no tock) and you switch into high matchmaking gear. Fearful that your days as a grandma will never come, and that one out of four of your grandbabies will suffer the wrath of "advanced maternal age," you begin to lower your standards. You'll start to think that missing teeth and college educations don't really matter. "But, honey, it's an eyetooth, not a front tooth!" And, "He's just street smart, not book smart."

This constant pushing will only make them resent you more and before you know it, your kids stop calling because there's nothing left to talk about when they meet you for lunch. This obsession to find them a mate drives a wedge between you that's bigger than a Packers fan's cheese-head hat. Ultimately, it may even be the demise of your relationship, one that you may never fully recover from. But that's the risk you take when you're such a "devoted" mother.

Martyr-in-Law

Once your babies finally meet someone they're happy with, they'll decide to take that trek down the aisle and become husband or wife. At the same time, you'll take on a different title as well, that of mother-in-law! Perhaps that's why you'll find yourself bawling through the entire ceremony like a widow at a funeral. Onlookers will think it's sweet how sentimental you are, but you know the truth. As your baby says "I do," you want to scream out, "No you don't!" "You can't." Or, "How could you do this to me?!" Watching your child take such a big step is like a sudden death of the innocent days of rocking your baby to sleep, singing him "Itsy Bitsy Spider," and holding flash cards of the various aspects of the solar system to instill a proper knowledge of planetary alignment. From this day forward, for better or worse, there'll be someone else standing between you and your baby. Yes, once your child has promised to love, honor, and cherish another person, you were relocated from the front row of their life way up to the nosebleed section with their acquaintances and coworkers, and you can't hold back the tears. All the bawling probably wouldn't cause such a stir if you weren't also wearing a dress that looked remarkably like the bride's. The lady doth protest too much (wide-eyed with surprise), "It's not white. It's *shell*."

It was hard enough when your baby moved out of the house, but this feels like he's moving out of your life. It's a new level of despair that sends you into an emotional tailspin. Now that your child is married, he'll put his partner's wishes above your own. Or at least he'll try to anyway. But you'll give him a run for his money that comes with years of Martyring experience. You'll buy them the dining room set and tell them how excited you are to give it a spin Sunday night at dinner. And the Sunday after that. You'll pay their way on a family vacation (far away from the in-laws) so you get them on most family holidays. Who can say no to "Mele Kalikimaka" and a mai tai wrapped in a giant bow? If you managed to hide grated green vegetables in his brownies, keeping your kid in your life once he gets married should be a breeze!

As a Martyr-in-law, you'll forever walk a frustrating line of staying important to your kids without pissing them off. You'll try to get them to take your side over their spouses' in arguments. (Warning: It is a known fact that if you try to force someone in love to pick sides, they will always side with the person they are having sex with.) You'll try to get them to call you on a frequent and regular basis. And you'll try to keep them safe by sending them newspaper clippings, magazine articles, and a shameless number of e-mail forwards containing the latest warnings and recall notices. You will try to squeeze in between them at every opportunity and, as a result, will become the most reviled villain since Hannibal Lecter. (In the first movie anyway. We found the sequel to be somewhat disappointing.) Your daughter or son-in-law will get chills whenever you drop by unannounced, just as you did when your mother-in-law did so to you. But that's the circle of life, my friend. A Martyr's circle of life anyway. A lifelong game of push me/pull you, of love and contempt, that will go on for years and years, till death do you part.

> But that's a Martyr's circle of life. A lifelong game of push me/pull you, of love and contempt, that will go on for years and years, till death do you part.

Congratulations, You're a GrandMartyr!

It finally happened! After all your not-so-subtle requests asking for one, your child has finally given you the ultimate gift of a grandchild (and you thought that pinch pot ashtray couldn't be beat)! After all these years, you have another malleable bundle of joy to love and mold. An empty brain to warp and corrupt! Oh, happy day! The only problem is its damn parents! It seems they aren't grateful for your unsolicited advice about proper parenting. Despite your attempts to the contrary, your child has developed a mind of her own and makes her own decisions. Damn them! Plus, she has a spouse that shares in her same skewed beliefs! They don't consult you on big decisions (what the hell is an osteopathic pediatrician?). They give your grandkid a name without your approval (a "family name" from the other side. Hmph!). They decorate its room in colors you object to (apparently "turquoise" is the new "pink"). Yes, the hand that rocks the cradle is the one that rules your world, and you're steaming mad!

Occasionally, when they're desperate for date night, you're granted a few hours of alone time with your grandchild, but you have to abide by their stupid rules. "We're weaning him off a bottle so you can only give him a sippy cup." "He's learning to use a spoon so let him feed himself." Oh, and that asinine one about letting him fall down so he can learn from his mistakes. You've never heard of anything so ridiculous. Thank God the kid isn't old enough to tattle or you'd really be screwed.

Once your grandkids arrive, it'll be a daily struggle to rule their nest. Despite the growing resentment from your child and her spouse, you'll keep trying. You'll give the kid a gorgeous outfit a week before Thanksgiving and say you can't wait to see him wear it to turkey dinner. You'll give the kid a cell phone for Christmas, regardless of the fact that you've been told in no uncertain terms not to (and we're sure you won't forget to preprogram your phone number as #1 on speed dial).

Your children are not going to be happy. They will tolerate you, but they will not enjoy you. You can explain how you did it all out of love until you're blue in the face, but the fact is that with every judgmental comment you make, every passive remark, and every deliberate attempt to control things, you will be backing yourself right out of their lives. You will find yourself reduced to holiday cards and Shutterfly updates. You will kid yourself by thinking that a Martyr/child bond is impossible to break. You will cling to the belief that it has been cemented by years of guilt, sacrifice, and dozens upon dozens of homemade cookies. Believing all of this will only make the fact that your kid wants you out of his life even more painful.

FAQs

We're sure after catching a glimpse of what your future holds, you're panicked and loaded with questions. Normally, you'd be given an informative Web site to explore that would provide answers and much-needed support. But we can't even make one of those sideways smiley-face thingies let alone set up a whole freakin' Web site. We wish we could at least give you an 800 number to call, but hey, those things don't grow on trees you know. So instead, we're going to answer the most frequently asked questions of a Stay-at-Home Martyr who's (finally) questioning her methods after catching a look at what her future holds.

Q: "With my kid finally out of the house, won't my husband and I reconnect again?"

A: We're sorry, dear Martyr, but after almost two decades of speaking only about your children, you'll find that without them around you have nothing left to say to one another. He's long ago stopped telling you about things that happened at the office, and you've long ago stopped pretending to be interested in anything he has to say that doesn't revolve around the proper care and feeding of your children. Yes, when your kids left home, it seems they took your ability to converse with your husband with them.

With nothing left to say, you'll become what you feared most: one of those older couples in restaurants who sit in silence throughout their entire meal. Back when you and your mate were young and in love, you noticed couples like this, not saying a word to one another, and felt sorry for them. You wondered how a couple could ever grow so far apart and swore right then and there that you'd never become them. But years later that promise will be broken and you'll be reading the *New York Times* (oh let's be honest—*Vogue*), sipping your café au lait, blissfully ignorant of the fact that there is a man across the table sharing the meal with you. And the mystery of how a couple can devolve will finally become clear.

Your sex life will have died years ago, too. Your plan

was always to wait until the kids got older and then turn on the charm. But let's assess that plan. You waited so long that (assuming your husband also waited and didn't return from a business trip with a bad excuse and a fresh STD) you have very little relationship left on which to build. Your three-times-a-week romp in the hay turned into once a week, then once a month, then seasonally. Now the closest you come to having sex is when you pass each other at the door and yell, "Screw you!" Gravity has also had plenty of time to drag down any perkiness you managed to hold onto post-children (both boobs and attitude). You have more wrinkles, less sex drive, more age-related weird skin growths, and come on, those Viagra commercials aren't "popping up" everywhere for no reason.

Face it. You and your husband are in desperate need of counseling. After so many years of chipping away at the foundation of your marriage, you're left with a lot of deep cracks that could easily grow into a permanent rift. Act now. Soon you'll have nothing left to say and no one interested in hearing it. Preserve your marriage before you wind up living in a house half the size, with a bank account half as full, surrounded by twelve cats ('cause he got the dog in the divorce), and a welcome mat that reads, THIS IS THE THANKS I GET.

Q: "With my kids finally gone, I should have plenty of time and opportunity to finally get my body back in shape, right?"

A: Wrong. It seems your marriage isn't the only thing that will slip away. So will your ability to look down and see your feet. If you never developed the motivation and willpower to get your body back into shape after you first had kids, it'll be even more of a struggle later. If you thought dieting and exercise were difficult when your kids were young, it'll be nothing compared with having to do it when you're older. Your metabolism will slow down, your activity level will drop, and you'll be clinically addicted to Funyons. Plus, after all those years, your layers of fat will have adhered themselves to your frame like barnacles to the underside of a ship.

Every morning you'll scan your closet deciding what to wear. You've kept your pre-pregnancy clothes all those years, convinced that one day they'd fit. You see them in the bowels of your closet mocking you like kids on a playground as you grab something with an elastic waistband yet again. Over the years your skinny jeans will evolve into relaxed fit and your midriffs into "tunics." You try to get motivated and head out to the gym, but you're intimidated by all those sexy young girls wearing spandex shorts smaller than your underwear while you're in chest-to-knee Spanx.

Losing weight is all about taking baby steps, and you'll have so many steps to take it'll be like walking to the moon and back. You're just a hop, skip, and a jumbo frank away from having to buy two airplane seats, and you'll feel like you're past the point of no return. Sure, there's always gastric bypass, and if you're into things like pain and rectal leakage, go right ahead. But the chance of a lifelong Martyr ever looking good in a cinch belt is as slim as Tom Cruise ever living down that manic, creepy sofa-jumping thing. Ain't never gonna happen.

Q: "What about my Martyr friends? Won't I still have their unconditional love and support?"

A: Not a chance. Martyr friends, like smoke detector batteries and Pamela Anderson's husbands, are replaced every few years. As your child grows and moves from elementary school to middle school to high school, you'll meet a whole new set of Martyr friends to cling to who will have children the same age and sex as your own. As your kids grow, your concerns change. Instead of swapping potty training advice and discussing the challenges of raising a lefty, the topics will grow along with the kids and revolve around how to get them into the right schools, the right crowd, and ultimately, the right rehabs.

Of course, like your Martyr friends before them, there will always be an underlying competition about whose kid passed the gifted test, whose got a scholarship, and whose got the lead in the play. But with the kids all grown up, you'll find you have nothing left to compare and contrast. Sure, you'll brag about your grandkids and keep the ladies up to date with your adult children's accomplishments, but no one will really give a crap anymore. You'll try to fill the dead air by talking about other points of interest like politics or the weather. You'll quickly realize that the only thing you had in common with these friends was obsessing over your children. And like a relationship that's only built on sex, it will fizzle and die, and you'll be left in one big quiet awkward moment where no one has anything left to say.

Q: "At least with the kids gone, I'll finally be able to take those long vacations and travel the world, right?"

A: Unless you plan on stowing yourself onboard or robbing a bank, the answer is no-can-do. After years of proper Martyring, you've blown your wad on private schools, one-on-one lessons, home tutors, imported clothes, laptop computers, upscale hair salons (for your kids at least), and European vehicles when they turned sixteen. Now that they've moved out, you still need to support them in the manner they've grown accustomed to. Private dorm rooms, new school books (no child of yours will buy used!), and three square meals plus a generous cappuccino fund.

If you've Martyred correctly, your bank account will continue to bleed dry since your child won't be able to find a job that they think is deserving of their skills. How could such a "special someone" take a menial job for minimum wage? You'll be forced to support your child forever since tough love is way too tough for you.

We're sorry, my friend, but the most international place you'll be traveling in the near future is your local Ikea. Pick up a bag of frozen meatballs and a jar of Lingonberries, and it's the next best thing to being there. This is the price you gotta pay for raising your child in the very best, and making him believe that he shouldn't settle for anything but . . . even if you're the one footing the bill.

It's Always Darkest before the Dawn
. . . .

We realize you might be scared by such dismal prophesizing. Now that you've seen what your future holds, you may be tempted to pull a Scrooge, dart to Dean and Deluca to buy Tiny Tim a giant, free-range, organic turkey, and leave it on his doorstep without so much as a "call me in the morning." Pause a moment. Take a breath. Stop buying overpriced items at high-end markets. It was all just a bad dream. You're still (relatively) young and you have a second chance at creating a life for yourself. We hereby grant you permission to be a little bit

You have a second chance at creating a life for yourself. We hereby grant you permission to be a little bit selfish. To do something fun or mildly indulgent even when there are more pressing things to attend to.

selfish. To do something fun or mildly indulgent even when there are more pressing things to attend to (i.e., homework, laundry, housekeeping, meal prep). We guarantee that the dirty clothes and unmade beds will still be there when you return. And the homework wasn't yours to begin with. When you have genuine friends, commitments, outside interests, and a husband who can't wait to get you alone, your kids will look at you with admiration and pride instead of insecurity and need.

You have a second chance at mothering as well. You can still cut that damn umbilical cord and give your children the space and autonomy they deserve. You can still love them and *want* to squish them and catch them and boost them

218
· · · · ·

up—just don't. Let them fall. Let them catch themselves. Let them mess up and cry and get mad at you for sticking to your guns. They will thank you later. Giving your child the gift of becoming who they are meant to be and not some warped version of what you imagined them to be is a gift that will keep on giving. As a fully realized, content adult, your child will welcome you

You can still love them and *want* to squish them and catch them and boost them up—just don't.

into his life and that of his children. Grandma will be that interesting, engaging, lively woman that little Xenon (from the Top 20 names list of 2040) can't wait to see.

"Mommy, when will Grandma be back from her Kalahari cyber safari?"

"Mommy, why doesn't Maadihsunn's [also on the Top 20 list] grandma take Irish clogging class like my grandma?"

If you redirect some of that energy back on developing yourself, you will ultimately enrich the lives of all around you, and feel a sense of peace and fulfillment you never knew through the accomplishments of others. The sooner you land your "helicopter" and let life unfold as it was meant to, the happier you'll be, your husband will be, your kids will be, your friends and family will be, and even poor Pretty Princess will be. It's not too late.

Epilogue

Congratulations! You made it through the book! We know it was hard seeing yourself in such an unflattering light. It's always hard to look at ourselves up close, and this wasn't just a regular mirror reflection, but one of those magnifying ones where each pore looks like a wading pool. You had no idea what being a Martyr was doing to your family. No idea the damage it was causing. But now you do, and you're committed to changing your ways! Good for you!

Let's take your newfound commitment one step further and make it legal! Better than legal actually. Let's pinky swear on it. Let's cross your heart and hope to die of something other than sheer exhaustion from raising your kids.

In recognition of your fine accomplishments, and for moving away from the dark side of parenting and into a lighter, more flexible, and more balanced state of mind, we award you this certificate (and no, this award is not for just participating, like the kind you *used* to want your kid to have). Display it with pride as you would any other well-earned award. You deserve it! With your newfound attitude, we wish you a lifetime of joy that comes from raising self-confident, able-minded, and independent children, and a marriage that stays together for love, and not just for the sake of the kids.

Raise your right hand and repeat after us (in a loud confident voice, not a meager whisper because your baby is asleep, behind closed doors, with a Sharper Image white noise machine humming to block out all peripheral noise):

Certificate
of Mommydom

I, [state your name, and no, not "Mommy," your legal name]
do solemnly swear to use at least 52 percent of this book, including:

- sleeping in my own bed without any offspring, stuffed toys, or annoyingly loud baby monitors next to me when my kid's just sleeping in the next room but I want to be sure to hear its every inhale;

- babyproofing only what's life-threatening and not what will inflict only a minor owie, thus teaching my child consequences to actions;

- leaving the house properly groomed, in stain-free clothes that are more expensive than what my kids wear;

- getting an outside interest other than my child to keep the six remaining brain cells I have left after pregnancy alive;

- nurturing a relationship with my husband that includes a regular date night, grown-up conversation, and sex on days other than anniversaries, birthdays, and ovulation days if I'm trying to conceive;

- making just one meal for dinner instead of a separate one for each person at the table; and, last but not least, not feeling guilty for putting my needs above those of my children on occasion, and knowing that by doing so, it will lead to stronger children and a better mom.

With the powers vested in us by M.A.M.A.R.Y.
(Mommies Against Martyrdom and Raising Youths-who-can't-cope), we now pronounce you "Mother," not "Martyr."

About the Authors

Joanne Kimes is the author of *Pregnancy Sucks* and nine other titles in the Sucks series. She has written for the Disney Channel, Nickelodeon, and FOX. Visit her at www.sucksandthecity.com.

Jennifer Worley left her position as V.P. of Creative Development at Radar Pictures to pursue her writing career. She has written on various feature films and has a graduate degree in Human Development with a specialization in Early Childhood Development. She lives with her husband, four kids, and needy dog in Los Angeles.